HOW TO BE
A CHANGE M

HOW TO BECOME A CHANGE MASTER

Real-world Strategies for Managing Change

Philip Atkinson

First published in 2005 by
Spiro Press
17–19 Rochester Row
London SW1P 1LA
Telephone +44 (0)870 400 1000

ISBN 1 84439 001 2

British Library Cataloguing-in-Publication Data.
A catalogue record for this book is available from the British Library.

Library of Congress Cataloging-in-Publication. Data on file.

Spiro Press USA
3 Front Street, Suite 331
PO Box 338
Rollinsford NH 03869
USA

Typeset by: Arrowsmith, Bristol
Printed in Great Britain by: The Cromwell Press
Cover image by: Nature Picture Library © Grant McDowell/naturepl.com
Cover design by: Sauce Creative Limited

Spiro Press is part of The Capita Group

To Ann, Sarah and Jonathan

Contents

Introduction

DEVELOPING INTERNAL CONSULTANTS TO DRIVE CHANGE

We live in increasingly uncertain times. To meet this challenge we need high calibre, committed and motivated people to act as expert 'internal consultants', willing to take on the confusion and ambiguity that has become the norm for most businesses. We need people with the charisma and authority to sustain, improve and reinvent our businesses. We need a special team of individuals to drive through change, at both a strategic and tactical level.

I am not referring here to a 'top team' or the leaders of an organization; such people are expected to possess the transformational persona to steer the organization through crisis and chaos. What I am referring to is a group of individuals *internal* to the business, people that the organization relies upon to bring about change. Whatever their job title – HR advisor, project manager or best practice co-ordinator – these 'internal consultants' are charged with driving improvement through the business in order to ensure a more secure future. Consequently, they need to possess the strength, assertiveness, sensitivity, behavioural skills and political acumen to champion and support the organization as they lead the transition – they need to be change masters.

CHANGE AS A CORE COMPETENCE

A key competitive differentiator in any business is its ability to develop and grow staff to lead the process of change. Internal staff already understand the organization; they understand its culture and its people. The wise business leader appreciates the need to invest in such people to drive change.

This book focuses on how to develop superior 'consulting skills' within your organization, so it can become adept at managing change. It is aimed primarily at the existing – or aspiring – *internal consultant* (though much of what follows will also be of interest to the external consultant). It is also aimed at anyone wishing to encourage the development of change masters within their organization.

I have worked in change management consultancy for over 10 years, helping organizations from every industrial and commercial sector. In this work, my colleagues and I apply the behavioural sciences to solve difficult cultural and organizational problems. When faced with such an assignment, one of the first things we do is ask top team members a key question: 'In terms of driving change, in which of the following categories would you place your people?'

CATEGORIZING COMMITMENT TO CHANGE – WHO FITS WHERE?

Enthusiasts – these people take on a challenge, becoming a champion for, and leading, new projects. They are not afraid to stand up and speak out when improvements are required. They are committed to 'Continuous Improvement'.

Early adaptors – these individuals may not volunteer to lead a project but are quickly inspired by the passion of the Enthusiasts. They eagerly commit their time and energy to new projects and are fast learners.

'Fence-sitters' – these people have seen changes come and go; they may be cynical about what they perceive to be the latest fad or 'flavour of the month' initiative. Their commitment is weak.

'Resistors' – these usually resist any change, in a passive manner. They find a multitude of reasons for not participating in a change initiative, and will always find a counter-argument or try and score negative points.

It is a sad fact that even in the largest businesses the same few names keep cropping up in the 'Enthusiasts' category. Often the top team can name as few as 8–12 people who fulfil this role within their organization.

Now, just imagine what such an organization could achieve if it were able to triple the number of its Enthusiasts within a short period of time? What would be the consequences for the business? How many more projects would be completed on time? What new ventures, currently on the wish list, could be installed smoothly? What impact would the possibility of being able to implement complex projects or changes quickly have on the rest of the organization? How much time and resources could be freed up? The benefits of pursuing such a strategy are obvious, and they can go straight to the bottom line.

Instead of complaining about the difficulty and complexity of introducing change, what if you had the right people to invite change as 'business as usual'? Wouldn't it be great if you could rely on a core of people with the skills and ability to revolutionize and revitalize the culture of your business, adding positivity, creativity and improved business results?

Such people may not be formally trained in consulting skills. They may, however, have had some training in problem solving or quality improvement, or the use of project management techniques as a methodology for change. They may even have had an HR, Training, Management Services or O&M (Organization and Methods) background – but no real experience of 'true' consulting. By true consulting I mean working with a variety of 'clients' on diagnosing core issues and then encouraging them to take ownership to formulate, sell and implement solutions.

My experience is that very few people have had the opportunity to hone their skills in other than technical tools and techniques. However, equipping them with a new set of behavioural tools and political awareness can substantially improve their personal effectiveness, and reduce any personal anxiety they may feel about fulfilling the change role.

SUPERIOR INTERNAL CONSULTING

For the last seven years my colleagues and I have been running workshops entitled 'Superior Internal Consulting' and 'Mastering the Politics of

Change', in both the UK and US. The content of these sessions, including the contribution of well over 1,000 delegates (primarily occupying the role of 'internal consultant' in leading businesses in the UK, US and Europe), is encapsulated in the pages that follow. I am grateful to these delegates for their insights and experiences; their contribution enriches all of the models and processes that will be explored as you work through the book.

THE FUTURE – ORGANIZATIONAL RENEWAL

Organizational renewal is central to survival. Having exceptional people equipped with the beliefs, values, methodologies, behavioural tools and political 'know-how' to implement change must be high on any business leader's agenda. This book focuses on how to capture this expertise – whether for yourself as an internal consultant or in your role to develop internal change agents within the organization. Those who will derive most value from this book include anyone tasked with driving through change, in particular:

- Internal change agents
- Trainers and HR professionals
- Customer Service and Quality managers
- Specialists of Continuous Improvement – whether in IT, Re-engineering, Manufacturing or Productivity Improvement
- EFQM (European Foundation for Quality Management), Best Practice, Best Value and Balanced Scorecard practitioners
- External consultants and Organization Development practitioners.

No one can predict how major political and economic events taking place today will impact on the business world tomorrow. All we can be certain of is uncertainty itself. We now live in an environment where events in one part of the world can have a profound impact on economies and businesses across the globe. No matter how hard we try to predict and control change, we will never be sure just how well we can control the consequences of major external events. Living in this dynamic and dangerous world demands individuals who are not afraid of ambiguity and who see adaptation to change as a natural challenge.

MASTERING AMBIGUITY

Most organizations employ too few people with the ability to manage change. Such people are in short supply; people with the ability to anticipate problems, confront ambiguity in circumstances of risk or uncertainty and diagnose and analyse how to implement solutions. Organizations starved of this talent will have difficulty mastering the complexity around them.

The single biggest challenge when preparing to manage change is investing in preventing failure to ensure success. In an uncertain world you need to anticipate major changes (and their impact on your business) and build enough momentum to establish self-correcting mechanisms. This does not happen by accident. It is not simply enough to have the commitment to respond to events. You need a special group or team that can rise above day-to-day problems and deal with the core change issues.

DRIVING CHANGE

When times get tough you would expect most organizations to react quickly and implement changes speedily. Our consultancy experience begs to differ. The ambiguity associated with change actually stultifies the average business. Decision making slows down and, in many cases, grinds to a halt. It is a strange phenomenon. The demands for change and improvement urgently require solutions to promote organizational effectiveness. But what typically happens? It seems that organizational change can put many people into a 'holding pattern' of activity, struggling for several months. This freezing or slowing down occurs because of a perceived uncertainty about how the organization manages ambiguity. Fundamentally, this reflects on the ability of the business to reinvent itself.

Organizations – in both the private and not-for-profit sector – need to respond rapidly to the changing expectations of stakeholders. Businesses that have not yet fully captured the skills and abilities of their most able employees are failing to fulfil their business potential, and that of their people. Tremendous opportunities are wasted. I believe that all organizations have a dual challenge – first to nurture and develop their people to drive, align and meet the change agenda, and second, to set them to work developing a self-sustaining culture that is designed to feed back its own performance and adapt to the times.

To date, these challenges have been ignored by many organizations. Too often organizations have relied upon the large consultancies to provide the answers. With recent scandals in the corporate consultancy world (eg the Enron debacle involving various consulting businesses), the big 'consultancy solution' is being called into question, and the trend is to seek advice from specific business experts. Organizations are demanding a totally tailored solution, but implemented by people who understand their particular culture. Although the use of business experts is a continuing trend, the focus is now on equipping the organization with the capability to implement solutions itself, thus becoming self-renewing. Organizations now want to transpose skills from the consultancy world into their own selves.

DO YOU HAVE INTERNAL CAPABILITY?

If an organization is not investing in using its people more effectively, and striving to improve, then it is probably standing still. If a business is standing still, chances are it is really slipping backwards. One question you should ask yourself every day is: 'Are we better or worse than our competitors at managing change?'

The purpose of this book is not only to outline some powerful ideas and approaches to achieving 'change mastery', but also to develop a powerful and sustained system for Continuous Improvement.

It concentrates upon three strategic imperatives for change:

1 Developing – as a core competency – the capability to create 'change masters' to drive change from within the organization.
2 Using behavioural skills and political wherewithal to create and refine a process of continual organizational renewal and improvement.

3 Applying the approaches to create a culture of self-renewal.

Business is becoming increasingly complex, and organizations that wish to survive will have to learn to be proactive and drive change, rather than be driven by it.

Change itself is accelerating, and many organizations are failing to maintain their ability to adapt at the required rate. Their future is poor. Consider the top 50 of the *Fortune* 500 US companies in the late 1980s. Today only a few with their original names and in the same industry even register on that list. Many no longer exist, having been merged into other businesses, been taken over or gone bust!

This is not a passing trend. For organizations to prosper and grow it is vital that they learn to master, rather than merely adapt to, their environment.

This book offers a variety of diagnostic and change tools to help internal change agents analyse situations and respond swiftly, and appropriately. A combination of these cultural tools and methodologies can be used to triangulate the causes of any problems; you can then act quickly to implement necessary improvement.

This book has been written for anyone tasked with mastering change. The aim is to give you the tools to drive through and implement change, whether acting as change master yourself or creating a strong internal team of change agents or consultants.

Focusing on the potentially more difficult side of the change process – the dynamics inherent within the business culture – the book comprises 10 chapters, which are best read in sequence. Each chapter concludes with a summary.

Change as a Political and Behavioural Process

'To understand change management one first has to understand that change is a political process, fuelled by diverse behaviours and motivations not always committed to the greater good.'

This book is for the internal 'consultant' or change agent responsible for driving change in any business. It focuses on understanding the nature and power of political and behavioural forces and the context in which they operate.

If we could simply follow a logical sequence of steps that guaranteed the successful implementation of 'change' then life would be easy. However, this would involve purely 'left brain' thinking (relying solely on logical solutions to complex organizational problems) as opposed to 'right brain' thinking that takes into account the emotions, motivations and attitudes of individual people. If change were that simple we could construct a simple cause-effect model and the change would be implemented by the end of the week! We know that the process of managing change is far more complex than this. Change has to take account of the 'people' factor, which includes the world of personal egos, emotions, attitudes, motivations, drives and behaviours. It is important to take a holistic approach to change, incorporating both 'left' and 'right' brain thinking. Change is a journey not a destination.

Why do people resist change so frequently, and so vehemently? Why don't they welcome it with open arms? Perhaps it is because we all tend to gravitate towards our own comfort zone – that area where we can be sure that our performance can reach the expectations of ourselves and others. When we stretch people beyond their comfort zone they become unsure of themselves; they question whether they can perform to meet the new demands and standards. This 'stretching' is often not pleasant, especially if it is you that is being stretched! Of course, stretching can be perceived as a positive – learning new things, experimenting, being creative and playful. But the reality is that sometimes we only experience its downside – the worry about living up to new standards, the concern that we won't learn fast enough. We doubt our ability to take thoughtful risks and are concerned about self-disclosure and what others will think of us. If this process of stretching – encouraging people to achieve more or commit to higher standards – is poorly managed then we can stop people in their tracks. They begin to think of the negative consequences of failing to live up to the new expectations and we soon encounter resistance. We need to focus more on 'right brain' solutions, where the needs, passions and motivations of people are engaged to support the change, rather than just focusing on the logistics of rolling out a new programme.

Consider this: according to many sources as many as 90% of major culture change initiatives fail.[1] Now consider the relative success of companies that have either merged with or acquired other businesses. In Europe and the US between 56–80% of mergers and acquisitions fail to achieve the synergies for which they were originally designed; they fail to integrate several business cultures into one new business entity.[2] The primary cause of this failure is an inability to encourage a corporate culture that supports the objectives of the new business entity. So what is happening? Why are change initiatives failing, and with such regularity? And what can we do about it?

Let's explore the main reason why change doesn't work as well as it could. It can be stated simply: we don't apply 'whole brain' thinking to the problem. As stated previously, there is a tendency to apply logical models for change (which I refer to as the 'rational-technical' approach) rather than 'right brain' solutions that engage people and their motivations, address their fears and focus on involving them as active players in the change process.

Historically, technical innovation – whether production technology for the manufacturing environment or information technology for the service industry – has driven change. When introducing technical change it was important that the technical solution actually worked. As a result, a large number of engineering approaches, based upon the logical sequencing of events, became the methodology for change. The 'rational-technical' school of tools and techniques was born. These tools and techniques performed well when installing a production line on the shop floor; they gained in credibility. However, there is now too much reliance on the rational approach, to the detriment of the people perspective. Change can be made to work better and be implemented faster if we take equal cognizance of the 'political-behavioural' perspective, using right brain thinking and solutions to develop a holistic approach.

CHANGE IS ABOUT MANAGING EMOTIONS AND EXPECTATIONS

An effective change process is as much about managing the emotions and expectations of those involved as it is about practical steps to implementation. We need a holistic, balanced approach to change. Frankly, many organizations still think that change can be implemented almost entirely by following the old 'rational' model with a bit of 'man management' tagged on at the end.

A balanced view of change introduces the political-behavioural dimension. When change does not occur it is often because the key actors in the change arena have failed to grasp this dimension. The reality is that few people in organizations understand the dynamics of personal and organizational change. In some businesses this area remains the sole province of the HR department. Let's be clear; those who manage organizations that fail to train their change agents and internal consultants in both the rational-technical *and* political-behavioural approaches are not allowing them access to the widest range of tools to ensure success.

CASE STUDY

RESCUE MISSION

Many years ago we had a client in the engineering industry. Before beginning our work in the company, my colleagues and I decided to review a change initiative that had been introduced unsuccessfully the previous year. Our diagnosis revealed the following; can you see any trends that are applicable to your business?

The company was being steered by its customers in the automotive industry to seek ISO (International Standards Organization) accreditation as a prelude to rationalizing the company operations and applying for EFQM. The company had been established for 70 years and produced components for the automotive industry. The top team had 'committed' to a Continuous Improvement programme. These were the symptoms of failure to change:

- At the launch of the programme only seven out of the 12 senior management team attended and they were all operationally based.
- Training and development was not taken seriously, with an appallingly low attendance rate at most training events and many last minute cancellations. All training was focused on technical problem solving.
- The only communication to the workforce was the setting of quarterly targets directly related to the price of the stock.
- All projects arising from Continuous Improvement had to be based on 'cost reduction' criteria.

Armed with this information I asked some searching questions:

- Precisely what did the company do to engage the emotions of its people in the change process?
- Were the benefits and the rationale of the programme communicated before roll-out?

- What specific behaviours were identified as moving the business forward?
- What action could managers take to create a culture focused on achieving results?
- Where would resistance to the programme most likely occur, and what action could be taken to pre-empt any negativity?
- What risk assessment was developed to ensure that all resources were used to best effect on this programme for change?
- Were targets consistent with the goals of the programme?

The above example highlights an over-emphasis on 'left brain' planning. You won't be surprised to learn that a majority of change initiatives are built around logical-technical solutions and methodologies, neglecting the fact that an organization is a complex organism where political motives and behaviours play a significant part in shaping business performance.

WHAT DOES THIS MEAN FOR THE INTERNAL CONSULTANT?

To be effective, internal consultants or change agents have to progress well beyond the simple tools and techniques of change. They must be able to read and diagnose the political forces at play. They must be able to read behaviours and, more importantly, assess the motivations that lie behind them. They have to work well with people who may appear, on the surface, to be supporting change but who, in reality, are opposed to it. Effective change masters must use all their abilities to persuade, influence, negotiate, educate, reason and assert, and be sufficiently resilient to bounce back and restart the process when required. They need to have a positive outlook and be able to work with a wide variety of people and personalities. They have to be brave and assertive when required – especially with their project 'client'. There may be times when they will need to take career-limiting risks with senior people, handle ambiguity and be resilient.

Working with people enthusiastic for change is easy. What is more difficult is working with people who are less committed to change; people who sit on the fence, being neither for nor against change. More importantly, well-trained internal consultants can handle the organizational cynics, the doubters and those vehemently opposed to change. They can coach their project clients to take more responsibility and become actively involved in the process. Equally, they can persuade and negotiate with those tasked with, or targeted for, working through the change – the 'implementers'. They will motivate these implementers to take risks and stretch themselves beyond their comfort zone. The role is a little challenging! I trust that what follows will help you handle these issues.

CHANGE IS A FLOW AND A PROCESS – SYSTEMATIC AND SYSTEMIC

Successful change occurs when the internal consultant has the knowledge and experience to realize when a change model is simply only a model to help map out a series of 'What if' questions. Effectiveness in using any model – logical-technical or political-behavioural – is dependent upon, and reflected in, the quality of diagnosis undertaken by the consultant before any intervention or action. This diagnosis should include observations and analysis of the relative political health and behavioural conditions of the organization. The consultant who has the diagnostic skills, the

Systematic and Systemic Change

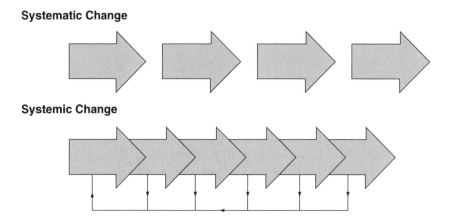

interpersonal skills and political insight creates a systemic process – one where feedback from observations and actions helps reformulate a model of reality that will work in introducing change. The rational-technical model for change is sterile and static. We need a model that is dynamic and systemic.

Imagine meeting practitioners of change and asking them; 'Did the old models work in practice?' Their answer may be, 'Some of them did, but only partially'. Sometimes it is difficult to determine what precisely caused what to happen. If we cannot be certain of precise cause-effect relationships in our models then how can we replicate the results in another part of the business using the same model? The internal consultant has to focus on developing cause-effect relationships. What 'effect' can you generate by 'causing' this specific action to occur? These are the issues that need to be addressed in order to develop a holistic model for change.

CASE STUDY

THE MERE ACT OF OBSERVATION CAN PROMOTE IMPROVEMENT

Working as a facilitator with the steering group on a cultural change initiative within a bank, my colleagues and I decided to hold our weekly meetings in the office of the Risk Management department. Our third meeting was interrupted by the manager of the section who announced; 'We know you meet in here regularly and word is that you are looking at the risk management process. We have met as a department and identified areas where we could speed up the processing of credit decisions. We'd like you to review our plan.'

This was a big surprise. The only reason we had held our meetings in the Risk Management department was because it had more space and was less noisy than other parts of the building. Our meetings had no direct bearing on risk management but it would appear that the simple act of doing 'something' could cause others to refocus their attention, and thus think and behave differently. This recalls the Hawthorne experiments of the 1920s in the US, when Elton Mayo's research revealed that the mere observation of people in organizations was sufficient to make them feel special, thus changing their emotional state from uninterested to motivated.

Some may say that paying more attention to certain aspects of the business merely encourages people to take an interest and become aware of potential problems rather than deliberately focusing on making change happen. However, the single act of focused observation may be more effective than any concerted effort to manage change using the rational-technical model.

CHANGE – FLOW OR SEQUENCE?

It is clear that an integrated approach to change models (see the five-stage 'Rapid Improvement' strategy, Chapter 3), that takes into account the actions, passions and motives of everyone involved in change, the deployment of human energy, potential resistance to change and learning and implementation, will be superior.

RIGOROUS ANALYSIS AND CERTIFICATION

If the body of knowledge attributed to the rational approach had been captured, and a methodology that worked even 80% of the time created, we would have developed hybrids of it by now. An example of the rational approach failing to achieve a simple cause-effect model is the obsession of many theorists with variants of the Balanced Scorecard, the Malcolm Baldridge Award and the European Excellence model. (The Baldridge Award was set up by US President Ronald Reagan to complement the Japanese Deming award for Quality.) The rational approach can be useful when initiating a project, but it is not possible to simply follow a model (applying it to all situations) then wait for it to work. Every organization is different. Several businesses have tried to apply the European Excellence model, and although it is a good tool and encompasses all the key elements to effect change, there are still vast areas where it will not work. These areas relate to shaping a strong and positive culture for the business. For example, although vision, strategy and leadership are perceived as being key to effecting change, the process of getting there (and the encouragement that causes the specific actions or behaviours associated with vision, strategy and especially leadership to awaken) is largely missing, assumed or generalized. The rational models of change fail to highlight specific actions to cause behavioural change, which is why there are still tracts of thought and actions (mostly behavioural and political) that have to be mapped in both the Baldridge and the European model.

A PRAGMATIC APPROACH TO CHANGE

Every business has a unique history, culture and background, and each operates in very different markets. Because every organization operates in a unique political and economic context the most effective change model for each business will differ accordingly. What works for a big City law firm in London won't work for a manufacturer of agricultural tools in Wisconsin. Some of the principles may be similar but the methodology, when applied, will make assumptions about the culture, politics and context of the business, and these will have a major impact on the success of the business.

KEY PLAYERS IN THE CHANGE PROCESS

The success of any change initiative, in any business, depends upon the effectiveness of the transactions and interactions between the key players in the change process. These key players are:

- those who lead or sponsor the change project – the 'client'
- those who actually have to drive through change and train or educate others – the 'internal consultant' or change agent

• those with whom they have to work closely to apply and implement the
  ideas into their work – the 'implementer'.

The interaction between these three sets of players is what makes
change stand or fall. No matter how well the technicalities of 'the change'
are mapped out in flowcharts or Gantt diagrams, these are only a start.
The real success comes from investing in, and orchestrating, these three sets
of players to pool their interests and work as a team, with overall
improvement in performance at the top of their agenda. How best to bring
the client, consultant and implementer together will be described later in
the book.

Understanding the conflicts that can arise in the change management
process – and knowing how to pre-empt them – is the key not only to
managing change but also to increasing the rate at which it can be
implemented. In our consultancy work, my colleagues and I have seen several
very large and successful businesses such as General Electric (GE) and Motorola
employing strategies for change acceleration. We have been successful with
Rapid Improvement (RI) strategies simply because we predicted where conflicts
would arise between the key players, and took preventative action. Businesses
that manage change successfully share a heavy commitment to investing in
the prevention of failure by planning for change.

This action is critical, but is often avoided if it does not meet the deadlines
of the rational-technical model. Interestingly, several clients have
commented to me that they cannot invest time preventing problems
because they have to respond quickly to current issues; they are always fire
fighting. It seems that once the train is running there is no way to stop it.
This focus on closure at all costs, and meeting lead times for project
completion (in spite of potential errors), is paramount in too many
organizations. This is particularly so when problems are treated with
temporary 'band-aid' solutions that cannot endure in the longer term.
When potential failure is highlighted, yet the urgency to complete on time
and fix problems after the event is the norm, the culture runs counter to
improvement. 'Band-aid' solutions only work for a very short time and the
original problem – that could have been fixed permanently but was ignored

– often escalates out of all proportion. Additional resources will be required to rectify what should have been right first time. These resources may need to be diverted from the change initiative. It seems that some change agents always take the short-term solution; they never have the time or energy to prevent a problem arising (and escalating), but they can always find the resources to go back and fix it.

A great deal of change implementation fails because issues and problems arising at the earliest stages are simply not addressed. Investing time in risk management, especially in relation to the client, consultant and implementer, has to pay dividends. I believe that many change initiatives do not accrue anything like the benefits for which they were originally designed because critical issues at the start of the project were not taken sufficiently seriously or were, in fact, ignored.

CHANGE IS EMOTIONAL!

Is that an understatement? Change, by its very nature, is emotional. Most of us deliberately focus on achieving emotional equilibrium, especially in our work. However, if we have to move out of our comfort zone we experience disquiet and disequilibrium. It is natural that we want to control our lives; when we feel we are losing control in any area we start to contemplate the personal implications of any change. At this stage we probably ask ourselves some key questions:

- How will this change impact upon me?
- Will it give me more control over my work, my aspirations and my life, or will it take it away from me?
- If I have less control over circumstances, are there potential threats to me, my role, my identity, my very continuation in the organization? How serious could these threats be?

Note the nature of these questions. The focus is 'me-orientated' and suggests that the thought processes are less, rather than more, empowering. The answers to these questions will tend to *limit* actions rather than expand them. As change agents cannot manage other people's emotions they may simply ignore their existence and impact, and focus more on what they *can* manage. In too many change initiatives people are over-managed, ignored, avoided or even marginalized.

Understanding how people may respond to change is a key factor in assessing to what degree any change will be successfully implemented, accepted and welcomed. Not surprisingly, most people's initial emotional response will be more negative than positive. This will do little to address and diminish resistance to the change initiative. We need an approach that engages all parties in the change, so that they feel part of it and commit to it, rather than resist it at every opportunity. We need a change model that takes into account the emotional response of people and assesses how we can better shape behavioural components to ensure that change is implemented effectively. Such a model also needs to factor in the political dimension of how conflict is managed between the client, the consultant (both internal and external) and the implementer.

MANAGING CONFLICT

The study of conflict is an area avoided by many change theorists, yet conflict is endemic in organizations. The very nature of organizations, peopled as they are by individuals and teams with different motivations and loyalties, suggests not only competing interests for resources but also for attention, status and power. Most businesses have developed a combative stance with conscious or unconscious competitive drives for control of resources, people and the culture itself. Conflict is a natural by-product of competing interests (healthy competition or otherwise), and yet in the main it is ignored. Conflict is perceived as a negative force, and yet it can be an incredibly creative force in any business, provided it is managed. The presence of conflict indicates that there are differences of opinion, approach and priorities that have to be resolved. Declared disagreement therefore is the first step towards positive resolution. Again, the rational-technical models ignore conflict, or rather they develop methods for containing any conflicts that arise. Many organizations are so stifled by unhealthy 'conflict containment' between managers, teams, functions, processes and specific locations and geographies that they expend more energy on protecting and defending their interests than they do on expanding their business.

CASE STUDY

CONFLICT CONTAINMENT

Working with a financial services company, my colleagues and I were tasked with developing a coherent customer focus strategy across the whole business. The idea was to concentrate upon those staff who interacted most with customers and influenced customer purchasing decisions. It was agreed that we would devise a special strategy for the 95% of people who never met the external customer, but were supposed to support those that did.

During our initial research we were appalled to come across such bitter conflict between 'support functions' that it was surprising the company retained any customers at all. Several support functions clearly went out of their way to create petty problems for other sections of the business. The whole customer management process – from initiating customer interest to closure of sale – was fraught with conflict and resentment. It appeared that points were being scored on some psychic notice-board, with winners and losers being proclaimed behind closed doors. The whole negative 'blame' culture was reinforced through stories of battles, heroes and villains that had been played out years before most of the current staff had ever worked in the company!

Over the years this organization had developed very different cultures that were functioning outside the parameters of strategic intent. An alignment was required which started with a swift cultural intervention; it was not painless. Certain people had to go – especially those who sustained the negative culture through negative behaviour. By performing this necessary 'surgery' the culture changed overnight. It was important to get the conflict into the open, and use it as a powerful tool for building a new culture based upon company-wide customer focus. The process started with the top team addressing small cross-functional sessions in the business, talking simply about 'win-win' relationships and how critical these were for the future.

A change model that fails to take account of the political and cultural dynamics of a business will fail to harness the real forces behind moving from a current to a 'desired' state of functioning. Conflict is a powerful positive force, if managed. Because conflict, by its nature, is a cocktail of mixed emotions, many managers feel they cannot deal with it. Failure to train managers in the behavioural component of change may lead them to focus on conflict containment instead of conflict management. Such managers prefer to control and contain conflict rather than use it as a learning vehicle for improving the culture of the whole business.

Few change models attempt to gauge and measure the key drivers behind the culture of the business. Failure to do this, however, creates major problems when any specific change initiative encounters a 'cultural road-block'. Diagnosing the culture of an organization is critical when undertaking a risk assessment of the effectiveness of any change initiative, yet it is an area where many organizational leaders feel out of control.

FORCE FIELD ANALYSIS – DIAGNOSING CHANGE INHIBITORS

When developing a holistic approach to change management it is wise to identify the dominant factors that support any change initiative and differentiate these from anything that may inhibit change. A simple model – 'force field' analysis – is a powerful tool for highlighting and identifying the major technical, behavioural and political forces that support change. The process follows a number of steps:

- Clearly understand and articulate the desired state to which you aspire and clearly delineate where you are currently in relation to the achievement of that state.

- Thinking of the 'current' rather than the 'desired' state, brainstorm a list of forces that support you in moving forward. Distinguish these 'helping' forces from those that stand in the way of progress – the 'hindering' forces. After identifying these two sets of forces, rank order them, from most to least powerful in both *helping* and *hindering* change.

Accepted change management practice may suggest – incorrectly – that you should identify those areas that are most powerful in pushing you forwards, and increase the relative intensity of these helping forces. Devoting more resources to these activities, and saturating the organization with their positive influence, will, many believe, diminish the relative power of the hindering forces. For example, this could mean devoting more time to training, developing a new strategy for communicating to the workforce or reformulating a leadership programme. However, the opposite effect occurs. Increasing the intensity of these 'helping' forces actually triggers even stronger hindering forces! So, for example, no amount of training or designing of a new leadership programme will reduce resistance to change from senior managers (maybe a key identified hindering force). Instead, the best way forward is to devise strategies for eliminating whatever causes or strengthens the hindering forces. Therein lies the secret to change; stop pushing with good intentions – believing that their sheer strength will diminish the forces that hinder change – instead remove blocks to progress first.

Critical to any change initiative is the ability to assess where the organization currently stands relative to its desired goal. Failure to assess the current state and health of the organization means that those who have to facilitate progress don't have a true bearing on the readiness of the organization to change. Without conducting this analysis, any resources or time spent implementing change may be completely wasted. Later in the book (Chapter 6) we will explore methodologies that can help with this process and support those who occupy the role of internal consultant or agent.

POLITICS AND THE READINESS FOR CHANGE

Be aware of any political signals about an organization's readiness for change. There may be signs that all is not well, revealed, for example, in the failure of senior staff to attend critical meetings in the change process. What message does this convey? Consider the example of a senior manager agreeing to give an opening address to a training workshop but who fails to turn up or is represented by someone more junior. What signal does this send? We all take away a 'message' from the actions – or inactions – of others in the change initiative.

READING THE CULTURE

Internal consultants need to look beneath the surface of an organization and identify the core driving forces that shape its culture. When we explore the deepest level in a culture we discover the presence of a 'belief system', the hidden drivers that initiate behaviour. Beliefs, often unstated, are ways of thinking about what the organization stands for and how it should do business with its customers, staff and suppliers. These beliefs were originally established by the creators or owners of the business and then shaped by events, personalities and circumstances over time. Beliefs are passed on in stories and legends and are incorporated into management styles; they are often unstated. They may not be written down in any codified form but people are well aware of their boundaries, how these beliefs are rewarded and enforced, and the penalties for non-compliance. These beliefs, although apparently not visible to outsiders, and even customers, are nonetheless very real and manifest themselves as corporate values. To avoid confusion, I delineate these values into two pure types. There are those that are 'stated' and codified in some form, reflecting what is important to the organization about how it transacts business. Values can often be written and communicated inside, and sometimes outside, the organization. There are also 'unstated' values, values that are so inherently engrained, and so strong within the culture, that people can be unconsciously aware of them but unable to articulate them with precision – we don't *think* them, we *feel* them.

To illustrate the point, remember growing up in your family? You didn't need to have a mission statement or the family values articulated and debated at a meeting. You just 'knew' what they were. You knew when you were living those values and when you were in danger of violating them. Sometimes there were warning signs of potential violation – the disapproving look of a parent, the tone expressed and conveyed within few words. You knew what was valued and what was not, you knew the cues. This is exactly the same as 'knowing' unstated corporate values, without being able to recite them by rote.

By working through the values – stated or otherwise – you can get a good feel for the dominant culture of the organization and the political process that supports and feeds that culture. However, beware of ambiguity. Incongruity confuses people where stated values are not a reflection of the real values. For example, the stated values may be 'customer delight' but the real values are volume and quantity of sales not quality of service. This creates an interesting paranoia in those who work in the business – they know that there is a fundamental incongruence between the 'espoused' values and the 'real' values. Understanding and exposing the values of an organization is key to ensuring that you start working from where the organization really is, not from where it thinks it is!

POWER COALITIONS

Where do the power coalitions lie in the organization? Who has the power to influence decision making and to decide resource allocation? What processes exist to support these two areas and who controls them? You may want to assess where the key decisions are taken. Who, more than anyone else, has the ear of the top team? Who supports whom? Understanding how key players work together is critical. Sometimes power coalitions are based upon rational business reasoning, but often they are based upon the personality of top players or those aligned with them. Remember, people like people like themselves, and personality dynamics are sometimes so strong that they bind people together in less than rational alliances. Similarly, the dislike of a particular person or personality type may be enough to marginalize some people more than others. It is advisable to spend a considerable period of time working through the likely personality dynamics of key players because these are central to how change can evolve and be implemented. Knowing how to deal with, influence and persuade these players is central to managing change. There are a number of useful typologies of personality development. In my work, we use a variety of models. A working knowledge of the personality dynamics developed by various psychologists, including Myers Briggs and Cattells 16 Personality Factors, is of great benefit to consultants.

POWER AND HOW IT IS EXERCISED

What is the source of power or control in the organization?

There are several classifications of corporate cultures ranging from Handy's[3] four Typologies (Power, Role, Task and Person) to Raven and French[4] classification (still the most quoted) which is outlined below.

POWER AND HOW IT IS ORCHESTRATED

Without focusing too much on any one school of thought, power in organizations can be considered under the following classifications:

Legitimate or Positional power – this form of power recognizes that power is legitimate to those who work in the organization. They have internalized the values and fundamentally agree with them. People feel obliged to fulfil a psychological contract with the organization of 'give and take'. There is a shared belief that individuals in senior management positions have got there through playing the game, the rules of which are shared by the majority of people who work in the business. The challenge for such businesses is to develop mechanisms to ensure that new recruits quickly come to share the same values, thus maintaining them for the long term.

Expert power (knowledge and information) – experts possess knowledge and information, that is the basis of their authority. In order to retain power they must maintain credibility with those that depend on them. In an organizational context, people may hold their position because of their functional knowledge. However, increasingly 'expert power' has moved beyond a functional specialism or specific discipline to operate across boundaries and organizational processes. People who are valued the most may have technical expertise but they may also have the ability to develop a 'helicopter view' of change. Experience in a variety of fields will often add more credibility to a person's reputation than that traditionally associated with detailed knowledge of a particular area. There is increasing evidence that many organizations are valuing and rewarding those people who endeavour to become experts across the whole organization rather than in just one area.

Reward power – this is based upon the ability to reward desired behaviour, and to do so in a legitimate, positive manner rather than through coercion. The desirability of the rewards – and the degree to which they are achievable and linked to behaviours – is critical. There is an expectation of an exchange between those who bestow the rewards (eg pay, conditions, status, choice of assignments, flexibility, promotion etc) and those who seek the rewards. This form of power only really exists when those who manage have the power to dispense the rewards. As soon as rewards are distributed randomly, without reference to achievement, the power of the culture declines because there is no associated relationship between the effort expended and the desired outcomes received.

Referent and Charismatic power – this arises from people wishing to refer or aspire to the person in a position of power. Identification with the person – and a replication of that person's actions – may be a guiding force in shaping organizational behaviour. For whatever reason, we gravitate towards people who possess certain characteristics and display desirable traits. Charismatic leadership may be a motivating factor to those who wish to emulate the behaviour of senior people in the organization. Businesses that rely upon the 'leadership persona' may be using referent power effectively. Whole business cultures can be turned around to perform more effectively if people can be convinced that a particular type of manager or personality is preferable to another. For example, the desire to create transformational leaders in the business is founded on the knowledge that real leaders are more than mere administrators and managers of processes. Real leaders practise a can-do, action-focused, team-driven, change-orientated style of leadership. They create role models that people associate with desirable traits and behaviours.

Coercion and sanction – the foundation of this is fear. Certain people in the organization have the ability to administer punishment, make threats or create difficult circumstances if they so wish. 'Hiring and firing', 'blocking promotion' or 'creating sanctions' in organizational contexts are examples of coercion and are usually associated with being the last ditch means to ensure compliance with the wishes of the business. Although people expect some sanctions to be in place, the degree to which they consider such 'coercion' to be fair is not just bound up with how any sanctions are applied but also with the reason why, and the criteria by which, they are used. The more an organization relies upon this form of power the less opportunity there is to motivate these same people to commit to change or improvement in a positive manner.

Issues on the power base – no one form of power will dominate in any business. Indeed, even in smaller parts of the organization several forms will manifest themselves; however, one or two of the pure types discussed will tend to dominate. Be aware of how these 'power bases' influence the behaviour of people and the retention and development of staff.

REWARDS AND PUNISHMENTS

The study of political life in organizations could occupy several books, but suffice to say it is critical to understand this area in order to assess where change will work easily, and where it will not. At no point would I suggest getting involved in political machinations, even to further the cause of successful change. However, I would suggest that consultants use their political and behavioural knowledge both to understand their project clients and to influence those who are open to change and those who will actually implement the ideas into the business. The real issue is influencing with integrity. I do not recommend using any form of political leverage to strengthen an unjust position.

CHANGE MANAGEMENT BEST PRACTICE

There can never be one definitive change process that always works, but it is useful to analyse the approaches that successful companies have applied to their own cultures. GE (General Electric) is one of the world's most successful companies with double digit profits recorded for the last 16 years. It is one of few companies to have undertaken studies of what really works in change management. In the late 1980s GE, having commissioned leading American business schools (Harvard *et al*), synthesized a model of change referred to as the 'Change Acceleration Process' (CAP), wherein both technical aspects of change and behavioural techniques were combined. This seven-stage process was the methodology for bringing about large-scale change within the company, and there were few parts of it that failed to follow the process successfully. It is indeed an excellent process. Having applied and worked with the CAP for over 10 years in different parts of GE, in different industries and different locations, this process has given me a deeper insight into what works in what contexts. The key issue that GE really came to terms with was the importance of changing the organizational culture to one that supports and is structured for change. For a business to build an infrastructure to support a continuous drive for improvement displays a powerful commitment to change.

The CAP has enabled GE to surpass its excellent record, not only to perform in a variety of sectors but also to grow its businesses organically. It also uses the process to help acquire – and quickly integrate – other businesses. While most organizations in the process of merging or acquiring leave much of the cultural integration to chance, GE focuses on specific 50, 100, 200, 300+ day integration goals and works on getting the culture right first. I find it hard not to praise GE because what they have achieved by simply focusing on action and implementation is impressive. Experience of GE and other like-minded businesses which refine and use emerging tools, techniques and methodologies has enabled me to rethink my original training in Organization Development and my approach to change management. From this has evolved a more holistic approach to change as process and flow rather than a sequence of steps.

SUMMARY

The combination of rational-technical and behavioural-political approaches to create real emotion for effective change is key. There is often an over-emphasis on problem solving, decision making, quality improvement tools and techniques, as if their application alone would result in improvement. Mastering the flow and process of change is the key. Change is systemic; after implementing an action we have to test its results by answering the question: 'Are we nearer or further away from our goal?' The second question is: 'Knowing what we know, what action can we take to keep us, or get us back, on track?' Adopting a systemic approach to change is more realistic when we have to manage the conflicting motivations and aspirations of all key parties. There will be greater awareness of what is happening around us. Greater knowledge provides a wider range of options and more leverage for change.

- Change is a political and a behavioural process. Failing to understand the dynamics, pressures and interactions in organizational change leads to failure.
- Change is more than a technical-rational-logical process. It involves engaging the emotions of people and, therefore, any change model must take this into account. It is not enough to change people's minds, you must also change their hearts.
- Change is a flow, a process of events, incidents and exchanges, not merely

a sequence of 'nose to tail' steps that can be rationally explored through a flow diagram.

- Methodologies such as the Malcolm Baldridge or European Excellence models give only a partial diagnosis and understanding of the complexity of cultural change.

- To understand the change process is to understand the role, aspirations and interactions between three key sets of players in the process – the project 'client', the change agent or 'internal consultant', and the people being targeted to apply the change, the 'implementers'.

- Focus your analysis on risk management, assessing any areas that could inhibit effectiveness; then act to invest in preventing problems.

- Change itself is a cauldron of emotions; the role of the change master or 'consultant' is to manage these emotions.

- Conflict is endemic and needs to be at the fore in order to better manage the process of change. You need to try and expose and resolve conflict between individuals and groups rather than devoting time and energy to containing it.

- First remove what hinders change and allow the 'helping' forces to take over. Increasing the intensity of the helping forces simply triggers yet more resistance to change.

- How prepared for change is the culture? What state of readiness for change exists within the organization?

- Corporate values tell us what we need to focus upon. What do your stated or unstated corporate values say about your organization?

- Politics and power – where are the power coalitions within your organization, and how does their relative control over resources and decisions influence your ability to implement change?

- Establish who you believe to be real change masters in your industry sector, and benchmark yourself against their best practices.

2

The Impact of Change

This chapter focuses on the consequences of failing to change quickly enough in today's frenzied economy. By highlighting these consequences we can use the 'pain' of not changing as a spur to commit to change. One of the key reasons for failing to manage change is failing to bring together all the key actors to create a 'change mindset', with everyone focused in the same direction. One of the main reasons that change programmes fail is due to incorrect 'assumptions' being made at an early stage, and the failure of the key players (especially the client and internal consultant) to align their direction, motivations and plans for bringing about change. If you have ever filled the role of internal consultant, reporting to the client, you may be aware of 'Pontius Pilate' syndrome. This syndrome is easy to understand and most people who attend our workshops nod in agreement as we talk it through.

This is the usual scenario. Before clients fully understand the role they should play in the process of change as project host or sponsor they reassure the consultant that they have their full backing. However, they do not understand or take their own responsibility seriously. They may reassure the consultant by saying 'Please phone or call in at any time' or 'My door is always open'. The reality is, however, that the consultant is now all alone – the client has washed their hands of the affair. That is the last the consultant sees of the client until the next review meeting. What is important at this stage is that the consultant is under no illusions. The responsibility and ownership for change resides squarely, and solely, with the consultant. This critical issue needs to be explored in depth and resolved speedily if any change is going to be effective. Also at this stage we need to look at the consequences of failing to change in a fast moving, dynamic environment.

We need to explore any 'life cycle' properties of the change process, in particular the importance of looking at the relative maturity of the business and the need to pursue any change 'agenda'. In very much the same way as the life cycle of products is examined (from initial idea through development to launch and decay), so there is a need to explore the life cycle of the organization (from vibrant emergence to decline) and its culture, using diagnostics to examine precisely where it stands in terms of change management.

Let's consider the role of the internal consultant and how it compares to the external consultant. Acting as an internal consultant is a great deal more stressful and anxiety provoking than being an external consultant. The pressure of driving change and influencing the roles and responsibilities of others and the distribution of resources can have severe career implications for the internal consultant. In fact, the internal consultant often has to be more resilient than any external. The external consultant can walk away after a project is finished, the internal consultant may have to renegotiate a new role for him or herself.

ARE WE CHANGING FAST ENOUGH?

Being able to implement change is central to the effectiveness of an organization. If the ability to change is so important why then do we not ensure that, when change is introduced, it is completed within a short time-frame? Why drag it out? Why is it that so many change initiatives start with a bang and end with a whimper? Why is it the case that enthusiasm for change is greatest at its launch but fizzles out as the programme rolls on? Part of the answer lies in the degree of planning undertaken between the two key actors in forging a 'change mindset' – the client and the consultant. If these actors fail to galvanize the mindset for the whole business, and fail to develop a plan by which progress can be assessed, what hope have those who are not privy to the design and focus of the process to ensure that change is implemented effectively?

As previously stated, change can be emotional! This can be particularly so for those who are less than supportive of any change. Consider the four types of people discussed in the Introduction.

Change Acceptance Curve

The 'Enthusiasts' will be first on the change 'Acceptance Curve' (see above diagram), followed in turn by the 'Early Adaptors' the 'Fence-sitters' and the 'Resistors'. The real problems for the client and the consultant are not the first two categories of people, but the second two, the Fence-sitters and Resistors. These folk are more negative and probably less trusting; they will require more time and resources to be convinced that change is in their best interests. Not surprisingly, the energy of the consultant is consumed at a much higher rate when dealing with these people. Think about their motivation; there is a good chance that they will be quick to jump on any errors, especially if any change is not seen to be planned.

CASE STUDY

READY, AIM, FIRE

Working with a colleague in a UK retail business in the mid 1990s I occupied the role of external consultant, working closely with the company's internal consultant. My colleague and I were charged with designing a programme to roll out to the whole business, starting with the top 80 people in the company. Because the company was very sales and retail orientated most of those attending our sessions were destined to become trained as trainers to roll out the customer service culture within each of their geographic areas. We had devised a plan for roll-out which involved several days' training in 'Customer Focus' and then a short three-day 'Training the Trainer' event which included material on presenting as a training team. Those participating in the event would then have the materials and the structure to work in training teams, spreading the concept throughout the organization. All the materials were printed and bound in packages. Handouts were prepared, checklists were completed and support materials put in hand. On the day of the launch the HR Director (who was one of the client group) launched the event with the first group of people. Everything went fine. The presentation and launch were well presented, until the HR Director left the session. Now the participants' real views were expressed!

About 30% of the course participants started to question us about the focus and potential benefits of the programme; clearly they had not been briefed by their manager or functional/regional director (who were all part of the 'client group', being members of the original steering group). This diverted us off course; the content and structure of the workshop was stopped in its tracks as we explained the rationale of the programme and the precise benefits for which it was designed. At this stage we had several Fence-sitters and Resistors present who informed us that they had seen this all before. To them it was just another quick fix that would disappear in the next six months, and it was something that would divert them away from their day-to-day work and priorities. You can imagine the rest of the discussion. This whole incident was symptomatic of the 'Ready, Aim, Fire' attitude of some of the client group, where the purpose, benefits and advantages of pursuing this drive were clearly not articulated to the 'implementers'. Just imagine if these people, left uncommitted to and unconvinced of the programme, were then tasked with cascading it down to their direct report and the teams that worked with them – how effective would the overall programme be as it spread through the organization?

In this particular case we did manage to avert disaster, and took preventative action for all future programmes. We both personally phoned all the participants for future programmes and quizzed them as to how well they had been briefed about attending our events. We managed to bring those people with no briefing up to speed so they knew the purpose and benefits of attending. Their motivation and commitment to the programme improved because they were now briefed accurately and fully before the event; they felt involved. We learned much from this experience in terms of testing and retesting for understanding – not just with participants but also with the client group – and about communicating the right message. This is now the key issue we work on prior to attending any event.

The story told in this case study is not unusual. Often what starts at the top of the organization as a thriving, stimulating programme ready to deliver results becomes diluted in terms of belief and enthusiasm as it reaches the lower levels. The reason for this dilution is a failure to commit at the early stages. At least 80% of corporate change programmes could be more effective if there was some investment in communication to participants before the roll-out.

ACCELERATING CHANGE

Every organization exists within a highly dynamic environment. Individuals have even less control than was thought. Consider the capacity of the average organization to master and install processes to support change; the ability to do so will determine its continuance in the future. As we move steadily into the first decade of the 21st century, today's organizations will have to acquire the capability to transform beyond anything ever known before, yet most organizations are doing very little about this. In order to meet the demands of the 'random' nature of the business environment they will have to change more in the next few years than they have in their whole history.

This change is not going to come about by accident, it has to be planned for and organized. We need to move beyond the rational-technical models for change that have dominated so much of organizational thinking in the 20th century.

Change is not constant; rather, it is dynamic. Most people do not realize that change is happening faster than their ability to adapt to the new demands on the business. Many companies do not have sufficient power over market conditions to command supremacy in their industry. They do not have the power and influence to move the market in their favour. They cannot shape the wills and intents of their competitors, or their customers, but they *can* shape their internal organization to win customer dedication and competitive advantage. This depends on their business awareness, their ability to scan the environment and to be self-critical about vulnerabilities and weaknesses in how they transact business.

CASE STUDY

VULNERABILITY ANALYSIS

Working with a top team in Financial Services, my colleagues and I focused our energies on Vision and Strategic Planning. The team had developed a business plan, had approved budgets and spending plans with their parent company, and had some good ideas for the expansion of new business. As is usual, when not everyone is always on the same page, a useful part of the workshop was having top team members question the assumptions behind the 'decisions' they were making. It soon became apparent that more time needed to be spent debating these issues and we broke for an impromptu session entitled 'Vulnerability Analysis'. We listed the key stakeholders and influences impacting on the business, including competitors, suppliers, trade journals, legislation etc, and then asked people to work in isolation on a series of questions.

In each of these areas, and for each constituent, stakeholder or influencer:

- Specifically, to what events or actions is your business most vulnerable?
- On a scale of 1–10 (with 0 as low and 10 as high) what is the probability of these events or actions actually occurring?
- What negative impact would these have on your business and your plans for the future?
- To what – in both the immediate and long term – would you have to commit in order to rectify problems?
- If you consider these events and actions to be high risk, what decisions can you take today to minimize any potential damage or remove the potentiality of these events occurring?

This exercise was critical in reshaping the future of this business. As you may gather, not all the top team were in agreement. We spent a considerable amount of time testing and retesting understanding and assumptions being made about the market and its key players as well as looking at functional, process and sales decisions from different perspectives.

Businesses are subject to the whims and foibles of economic, social, technological and geo-political forces. Successful companies will have to respond faster than the rate at which change impacts upon them. Advanced communications make the world a smaller place. Information flows faster, decisions need to be taken more quickly; organizations need to commit to multi-functional implementation in order to keep pace.

Too many senior teams fail to realize that the complexity of the business world is far greater than it was in the 1980s and mid-1990s. This is as true for the large multinational global player as it is for the small business operating from a single location. For the local player operating in smaller regional markets the ability to influence events will generally decline as new businesses move into the market. As barriers to entry in most industries continue to diminish, the very shape of many markets will change radically. This trend cannot be ignored from either a macro-economic or organizational perspective.

TURBULENT CHANGE

Who would have predicted the reunification of Germany or the demise of the USSR; who would have predicted the self-realization and determination of these countries?

To illustrate the complexity on an organization scale, consider this: what percentage of top companies in the 1980s are still in the 'Fortune 100' 20 years later? Less than 40%. Many of the companies in the current '100' may not have been listed in the earlier Fortune top 100 because they simply did not exist.

We are sure to see many structural changes in how we do business, far more in the next 10 years than ever in economic history; so what of the future?

WHAT IS OUR CAPACITY FOR CORPORATE RENEWAL?

So where does this leave business today? In the main it leaves top teams and senior executives confused. Confusion often leads to inaction and inconsistency, which leads to an inability to change at all. Effective change requires the ability to make and implement decisions confidently. As is so often the case, the complexity of change itself actually has a negative, draining effect on an organization's capacity to manage and transform itself.

Ambiguity in the environment actually slows down the ability of the organization to put in place the correct strategies and drive them forward. However, it is critical that this is done. Often, the ambiguity inherent in the operation serves to shut down all but the most routine decision making. This leaves the enterprise even more vulnerable to external threats.

Clearly this is a danger to the change process. Critical to this process is the attitude of the organization's top team and senior management towards the change process itself. Their actions – or inactions – clearly define the capacity of the organization to transform itself. People are 'boss watchers'; what the boss does and does not do indicates what is important or unimportant. Behaviour breeds behaviour in others.

WITHOUT LEADERSHIP THERE IS NO CHANGE

Those who run organizations are ultimately responsible for their ability to change and improve. Clearly, this is the responsibility of the senior team, and their teams of direct reports. I believe that the successful organization of the future will be characterized by a strong body of internal consultants or change masters who are equipped both to drive change and to manage their technical speciality to perfection. There is no trade-off between technical competence and change management. We need both to prosper in an uncertain future.

All this talk of change can be disturbing for the average organization. When talking about change, we need to appreciate that very few people really comprehend the complexity of the change process itself. This is why so many top teams prevaricate over 'changing'. They cannot leverage change because they do not understand, or know, how to build a high performance business culture.

To make matters worse, too many top teams simplify the processes of change, believing that following a systematic sequence of carefully boxed activities will yield the results they desire. This may help, but what top teams often forget is that change is a flow, a process with multiple feedback loops. The change process involves complex people interaction, making prediction of their behaviour in the organization almost impossible. Instead of understanding the softer elements of people, attitudes and behaviour, these top teams concentrate on the tangible and predictable. Unfortunately, by focusing on the tangible aspects of the business – the structure, systems and protocols – these teams control probably only 10–20% of the net effect in the change process. Organizations that focus on the softer elements of the culture are far more able to effect change because they control the 80% of the dynamics in the organization – how people lead, behave and work together.

A CHANGE MINDSET

A mindset of change, where transformation is perceived as 'business as usual', is critical to every business. But is this mindset living and breathing in the average business? If it is it must permeate from the top of the organization and flow through and across every function and over every boundary. It must be a process of flow. The concept of 'flow' is important because its constancy moves us away from the 'flavour of the month' strategies that characterize so many organizations' attempts to change.

CORPORATE LONGEVITY – LEARNING TO MASTER CHANGE

Only those who have mastered and control their business environment will be able to call the tune in the future. This will not come about by default, but can be achieved quickly by design.

LEARN TO BECOME A 'LEARNING ORGANIZATION'

The 'learning organization' is a term much overused, and misunderstood. However, a simple definition of a learning organization is 'an organization that develops its capacity to learn and implement best practice faster than the competition'. This is achieved through proper use of an organization's human resources. Organizations that employ the talents of their people to become change masters will prosper into the future. This book addresses some of the key paradigms, competencies, tools and techniques that will equip the organization to adapt more quickly than its competitors.

EXTERNAL CONSULTANTS

Many organizations, when faced with making strategic changes to their business, recognize that they need experts to smooth the transition. As the speed of change accelerated in the early 1990s so the consultancy business took off to meet demand. Business schools flourished and companies clamoured to employ MBA holders, believing that they were the key to competitive advantage. For some businesses, this approach worked; the bigger and more prestigious the firm the better.

INTERESTING CONCEPT, POOR INSTALLATION

Employing external consultants to diagnose problems can be valuable, but you need to consider their track record on actually implementing change. Implementation is an important issue, but installation (ie installing change and integrating it into the organization so that new practices are embedded) is critical. New ideas, methodologies and best practices cannot be introduced wholesale into an organization, they need to be inculcated into the fabric – the culture – of the organization. This is where so many academics and big consultancies failed in the 1990s; they focused on the quality and rigour of the theory rather than on the detail of the practice.

An alternative to working with the big consultancies is to work with a 'trusted advisor', the smaller 'cradle to grave' consultancies which work with organizations on several projects over time. These practitioners of change – who are single-minded and focused upon 100% implementation – are much in demand but few in number. There is, however, another alternative. How much better would it be if organizations had their own capability, in-house, to lead and drive through change? What if they had the opportunity to tailor solutions to their own needs?

TAILORED SOLUTIONS

Every organization is different; many forces will have shaped its business culture or corporate personality. The values that guide and drive the formation and development of a business will differ markedly. Charismatic leaders and influential people will have driven businesses in different directions. Changing ownership and economic, technological and political forces will all have made their mark. As organizations differ in their cultures so they will differ in which solutions work for them, and which don't. Therefore, in order to manage change successfully, organizations require individually tailored solutions. There is no universal panacea. Who better to tailor solutions than trusted advisors – internal to the business?

THE ORGANIZATIONAL LIFE CYCLE AND THE ABILITY TO CHANGE

The 'life cycle' concept is applied principally to products and services. We understand that every product has a 'product life cycle' (PLC) that tracks investment in the product or service and potential sales/profitability over its 'life span'. Simply stated, the PLC reflects the launch of the product, the growth of sales of that product, its maturity and decline.

Now, in the same way that any product has a life cycle, so too does an organization. Any business will go through defined stages; the route is summarized below (although there are other interpretations and explanations of the process). Let's consider the five stages in the organizational life cycle. The first stage is the 'Emerging' stage, when the business is first founded or created.

Organizational Life Cycle

The organization is probably driven by focused, entrepreneurial individuals who are keen for it to gain prominence in the market, attract customers and establish a strong identity. This is followed by the 'Expanding' stage; this may be characterized by increased momentum and growth in the chosen market. Entrepreneurial fervour is evident as is the enthusiasm, activity and rapid decision making that characterizes this exciting stage. If things go well, customers are retained and the business grows, there follows a 'Consolidating' stage when processes are rationalized and protocols set in place to deal with the economies of large-scale production. This should really begin as the business moves through the Expanding stage, otherwise the company may find that – although it is busy and in demand – the systems and procedures that govern service delivery are not sufficiently robust. This is a difficult stage to manage. On the one hand you are concerned with expansion and growth and on the other with a consolidation of processes. In extreme cases, sales people are out selling to new prospects and projecting the vigour of the business while, in the organization itself, a degree of bureaucratization is taking place. Meanwhile, as the business expands, the owners or creators may start to lose interest as what attracted them to create a business in the first place – the emotion, activities and risk – seem to be supplanted by process. It's all come down to routine.

It is at this stage that a significant shift in management style is sometimes demanded, from 'innovative entrepreneurs' to 'rational consolidators'. Moving from 'Consolidating' to 'Maturing' is a difficult phase. As the organization matures it can lose the sensitivity to changes in the environment that typified earlier stages. Now the organization can start to slow down, to simply keep up with what is going on in the marketplace, to become fat and happy.

ORGANIZATIONAL LIFE CYCLE – ACTIVITIES AND THREATS

Stage	Activities	Threats
Emerging	Innovative ideas Driven by Sales, Marketing Personality led	Differentiating the business from competitors Winning trust of initial

	High energy and activity	customers
	Risk taking	Delivering to expectations
Expanding	Developing a structure	Not expanding quickly enough
	Trusting in new people	Failing to gather the right
	Setting up initial processes	people around
	Running the organization as	Failing to delegate
	a business	The owners doing everything,
		demotivating starters
Consolidating	Winning customer loyalty	Not assessing wins and losses
	Expanding range of services	Taking things for granted
	Setting processes in place	Focusing too much on controls
	Bedding down the business	rather than new business
Maturing	Developing longer-term	Failing to develop customer
	commitments with customers	loyalty
	Agreeing systems and	Arrogance – believing too
	protocols for quality,	much in the brand
	consistency, reliability etc	Failing to pay attention to
		changes in the market
Declining or… Re-inventing	Maintaining trading in the same way Not aware of the impact of changes in the market Loss of self-critical faculty Slow to respond to change The organization becoming too large and impersonal Loyalty of staff not pronounced Risk averse	No review of progress – assuming the business is no worse than its competitors Staying in declining markets Failing to develop a new image and new products Expecting things to go back to normal
Re-inventing… or Declining	Organizational review Aware of vulnerability Re-emergence of self-critical faculty Hungry to change Cultural revamp Creating a performance culture Incentivizing change and improvement	Too much change too soon Believing incorrectly that everyone is committed to change Having some commitment but not the skills Trusting too much in external consultants delivering

DANGER IN THE COMFORT ZONE

This is a very dangerous period because if the organization does not have the ability to filter and predict the major changes in the environment – and take action to prevent problems arising – then an organization can go into the 'Declining' stage. However, if the management group are alert and have developed superior change management strategies they can go through the 'Reinvention' stage and revitalize themselves, and their business. They can then proceed through the stages again. On the positive side, it is an organizational learning curve featuring systemic change. The organization should reinvent itself continually; this is the true sign of change mastery.

If the organization is alert it will learn and develop from the 'Maturing' stage and move up a gear. If it becomes slow and takes things for granted it could well move into decline. This is precisely what happened to many companies in the UK during the 1970s and 1980s; they failed to take account of the increasing demand for quality and customer focus.

CORPORATE RENEWAL

As any organization grows it passes through several stages. Because every organization is different it is important to diagnose the exact state of the business before recommending change. Remember, one part of the business may be in decline while another is on the up. It is important that a precise diagnosis is made in order to develop a programme for change that suits specific individual businesses and their circumstances. No 'rational-technical' approach will be able to deal with the political, behavioural and emotional issues that are central to the culture of any business.

TAILORING SOLUTIONS TO WHERE YOU ARE NOW

In most cases a solution that worked for one business cannot simply be transplanted into another; it must be adjusted and specifically tailored.

External change agents cannot, by their nature and experience, drive tailored solutions alone. To meet the particular demands of the business culture, managers within the business must play a dominant part in driving the change process. Perhaps we could consider joint efforts where the external advisor and internal consultant work together closely to develop a body of change masters who can take charge after any initial and necessary external intervention.

GUARDIANS OF THE CORPORATE CULTURE

External change agents and business experts will always have their place in promoting and driving organizational change. Their expertise will always be valued as they have a part to play as objective observers and analysts in the problem-solving process. But the responsibility for change must lie within the fabric of the business. This does not mean that an organization will have a department of 'Organizational Renewal' or 'Organization Development'. This may be part of the solution but it is not the whole story. Creating a named department or function of 'Change Management' sends out clear signals to the rest of the organization that the responsibility for driving change rests with the experts in one area or with one function. This is a myth that should be shattered. Change resides with those who have to live with it – the line managers and eventually the line; the people who operate the business.

Responsibility for change should be owned from the top and cascaded as far down the organization as possible. It must be deployed throughout the organization.

WHAT SKILLS, ABILITIES AND MINDSETS MAKE THIS POSSIBLE?

The average manager or team leader is worked pretty hard by most businesses, but the real results for the business are only partly realized. Too often results are quantified by profitability, volume, cost reduction and delivery to specifications. Of course, these results are important because they reflect the ability of managers to transact business in their particular area of expertise. However, they lack balance and omit a crucial area of a manager's responsibility – how they can add value to the business in the longer term by creating a culture of Continuous Improvement.

In the business culture of the West we tend to focus too much on short-term results – usually to coincide with quarterly returns and Annual General Meetings (AGMs), to the detriment of longer-term goals. We know how important it is to return a profit to stakeholders in the short term. Profitability is the lifeblood of shareholder confidence; but what of the organization's ability to master its future? Short-term gains cannot be compromised but longer-term 'shareholder' and 'stakeholder' value can be achieved only by refocusing the contribution of managers, team leaders and employees alike to the need to drive and install necessary change. This means equipping managers and employees with the capacity to transcend the ever-threatening 'tomorrow' and start preventing problems arising in the future.

HOLISTIC CHANGE SKILLS

I would not encourage the development of still greater technical skills and competence at the expense of change management skills. Most people in organizations know more about the protocols, the detail, the production and operating processes than do their managers! We need to equip staff with the ability to manage change, so that a major part of their role is related to change management and Continuous Improvement.

At this stage it is crucial to understand that, without a major investment in developing a group of internal consultants, the average organization is only going to limp along compared to those that take the process of transformation seriously.

CHANGE IS 'TOP-DOWN', WITH A VISION TO BECOME 'BOTTOM-UP'

That's the way it starts. The goal or vision is that change will become 'bottom-up', with good ideas and implementation coming from all employees in a constant stream. It will become a flow, an energy where Continuous Improvement is a reality.

My belief is that Continuous Improvement is a goal and a process, it is the flow of activities reflecting the mindset of the leaders within an organization. Internal consultants should be driving this flow. They should be promoting Continuous Improvement as a philosophy, a mindset displaying certain attitudes and behaviours towards sustaining change.

Nothing changes until behaviour changes. The key to Continuous Improvement is to inculcate a culture of practical learning and curiosity into all levels of employees, in all functions and processes. That is Continuous Improvement.

SUMMARY

Change can be positively driven if we bring client and consultant together to form the central driving element of the change team, testing the assumptions that each is making about the conditions that underpin the change and the organization they are attempting to create. Where an organization sits in its life cycle is critical to understanding what will and will not work. The organization, its employees at all levels and its stakeholders all benefit from the change. The organization is maximizing the potential of its most creative people – and these people are genuinely contributing to change and reaping the rewards in terms of motivation and self-determination. The natural outcome is satisfaction for all stakeholders, and survival for the business.

- Central to effective change is the relationship between the person or team who owns the project and the internal consultant. These project owners, hosts or 'clients' need to work closely with those who will oversee and drive the installation of the programme – the internal consultants.
- Future business success is founded on the ability of the organization to transform itself – continuously.
- Organizations will need to change more in the next few years than they have in their whole history.
- Without leadership there is no change.
- Top teams should focus on improving the organization's capacity to transform and adapt itself to changing markets.
- Change is a process of flow, not a sequence of steps or stages; the style you adopt to adapt to change reflects your understanding of the process.
- There is no one theory of change that fits all situations or companies, although some 'experts' may suggest this is so.

- Change is complex – controlling the tangible hard elements of the culture will only yield 10–20% of results. Controlling the soft side – the behavioural issues – will yield 80% of success.
- Change is a core competency and a mindset, which should be owned and practised by all managers.
- Become a learning organization implementing best practice faster than the competition.
- Focus upon installing best practice; reject theory without action.
- Create an army of internal facilitators to become the guardians of your corporate culture.
- Always balance technical and change competencies. There is no trade-off in either direction.
- The vision for Continuous Improvement has to be top-down, with ideas and improvements flowing up.

3

The Internal Consultant
Developing a Methodology
for Change

The internal consultant must apply a rigorous methodology for change, and this must be 'owned' by the client. A methodology is a roadmap of the progression through each stage of the project or change; it outlines and lists the sequence of steps, the actions taken by the key actors in the change arena, the flow of energies and the desired outcomes. If the client and internal consultant agree the methodology – the process or framework being applied – then the job of the internal consultant is much easier.

Some organizations have a common methodology that dictates how projects or change unfold; however, many don't. For these organizations it is critical to agree such a framework so that everyone can understand where they fit in the process and the rationale for proposed actions. Failing to agree a change methodology may mean that the consultant will continually have to justify their approach. A flexible methodology should engender a 'common understanding' so that actors, participants and observers of the change process can all clearly see what is going on.

CASE STUDY

TIGHT VS FLEXIBLE METHODOLOGIES

Some years ago I worked with a large company whose major business was designing tailored software for a variety of organizations – mostly in banking and financial services. The company had developed a rigorous methodology based upon Computer Maturity Management (CMM) standards for IT software development. CMM as a standard originated with, and was perfected by, Motorola. As a methodology it guaranteed that the process undertaken to develop software was reliable, and that working through the process would always create the same results. Thus the process was 100% verifiable. The company was very proud of this rigorous approach and used a variant of it in all businesses dealing in the UK and across Europe. However, the company also believed that this same process would be of value when applied to other non-technical, non-manufacturing processes outside IT development. Unfortunately, the methodology was applied with the same rigour to cultural issues as it was to technical issues. There was no real match simply because the origins of CMM bore no resemblance to a methodology that would work for culture change; it just didn't work. What had been designed as an aid to software design was too rigid a process for anything else. Because the process had credibility and was so respected in driving the business forward, any criticism of it (even if not in the context of software development) was not taken kindly. The company needed to recognize that broad, general areas of a methodology need to be designed and tailored specifically to specific outcomes.

The existence of a methodology delivers clear benefits to a consultant because the 'process' already has commitment and resources to support its achievement; all the consultant has to do is create and ensure that the methodology and content of the change are integrated to deliver the expected results.

Some organizations extend their project management methodology or develop existing processes, such as for manufacturing or production functions, and apply this to change management. This can be an excellent start, but methodologies must progress beyond the technical elements of the approach. Creating an appropriate methodology requires the development of behavioural tools and techniques. These will add strength to a solid framework for change. Now the methodology should be able to address the cultural issues as well as the technical.

Developing a corporate framework or structure to suit the circumstances of the individual entity is important. Tailoring a change process has valuable paybacks. Some companies commit to this process, understanding that if a 'preferred methodology' is known and understood then the organization and its staff will know precisely the actions and processes that underpin any change. If your organization has not developed a methodology it might be best to commit resources to creating a process that is a framework for all change initiatives, whether technical or cultural in nature. It will pay off in the long term.

GE AND ITS CONTRIBUTION TO A METHODOLOGY FOR CHANGE

We can learn a great deal about the art and science of driving change from General Electric (GE). GE is one of the largest and most successful conglomerates in the world; it has always been committed to developing models for implementing improvement. Jack Welch was CEO of GE for almost 20 years, taking over in the 1980s. Welch inherited a large business that he considered slow to change. He committed to 'structuring the business for change' and in the late 1980s introduced a change management tool, later entitled 'Work-out'. Work-out was a concept that would infiltrate the whole business – from GE Aero Engines to Financial Services. Work-out, as a concept of Continuous Improvement, transcended the whole business of more than 300,000 people and brought about a major cultural shift. It created a common language for organizational improvement and was a forerunner of the highly successful methodology the 'CAP' (Change Acceleration Process), of which we will learn more later.

CASE STUDY

GENERAL ELECTRIC – THE PROCESS OF WORK-OUT

Work-out was a process that led to a continuous drive for improvement. It was based on three key principles: Speed, Simplicity and Self-confidence. The GE culture focused on Speed as the key competitive differentiator; it is the factor that permeates all change initiatives within GE. Welch had inherited a slow-moving culture in GE when he took over in the 1980s. GE was a huge conglomerate comprising many large businesses, some too unwieldy to be managed easily. Welch encountered organizations within GE that were just too slow to adapt. Furthermore, he was highly critical of what he saw as over-bureaucratization within some of the core GE businesses and claimed that these businesses devoted too much time and money to doing business with themselves. This is probably what inspired his mission to rid the company of slow-moving processes and bureaucracy. Welch coined the phrase 'bureaucracy is the enemy of change' to encourage people to make processes as 'simple as possible'. The Work-out concept was based upon developing a high degree of 'self-confidence' within the workforce. He famously argued that GE employed 'all the capabilities of their people just as much above, as below, the neck'. The commitment to promote 'self-confidence' in training workshops permeated the whole organization. GE was keen to develop a critical ability in its staff to examine and challenge everything they did, all the while looking for a faster, cheaper and better way. GE encouraged its people to rethink how they did things, to find a better way.

This was to be achieved through the focus on Simplicity, and included examining everything as a process. 'Process Mapping' became a desired problem-solving tool. Everyone was trained in its use to design sharper, faster, error-free processes, keeping these as simple as possible. It was discovered that managers applied too many 'checking' and 'inspecting' procedures. It seemed that no one had faith in some processes – they were checked and rechecked over and over again. This was a waste of time. The Work-out concept suggested that 'checking and inspecting' should be part of the work and process itself, not a separate function exercised only by managers. Managerial input was unnecessary if the 'process' did what it was designed for. It would be so much better for people to inspect their own work and be responsible for their own quality. No amount of inspection by managers would actually improve the process.

The GE culture was very much based upon replacing 'control' with 'trust', and this was a major factor in process redesign. All the time the focus was on doing and working 'faster than the competition' and doing things better and better; by cutting out wasteful and time-consuming practices the speed of decision making could be improved. By committing to Self-confidence and Simplicity, Speed was a natural result and organizations that had taken an age to reach a decision could now do so in half the time.

A few examples of how Work-out operates illustrate the rapid progress that can be achieved. Working as an external consultant at a UK location of GE Plastics, my colleagues and I managed to reduce significantly the lead-time for orders of ABS plastic. A large number of automotive companies purchased ABS plastic for making cockpit components, bumpers etc. GE were tasked to reduce the customer order to delivery time. Using Work-out, and harnessing the commitment of the workforce, the process was redesigned to facilitate turnaround from order to dispatch to three days instead of the usual 90! Through careful analysis the workforce was able to reduce the lead-time by 87 days. It took us about three months to undertake the analysis and design the new process, test it and put a new inventory management process in place. The results were staggering. Just imagine the effect on worldwide operations of using Work-out as a cultural tool for bringing about performance improvement. Just imagine how Work-out has improved business performance for GE. Think about what impact Work-out could have on the average organization, and on your organization.

The success story doesn't end there. Working with GE Capital (Motor Finance) we managed to remove 18 unnecessary steps from the credit scoring process (the ability to test the credit worthiness of customers). This saved significant time that was then devoted to developing an online credit scoring system. Now 97% of proposals for finance are approved online in just four minutes! Go to motor dealerships that don't use GE as a source of financing vehicles and you could wait days for an acceptance. Just ask yourself, would you be attracted to doing business with a company that can get a firm Yes or No to your finance in four minutes or would you prefer to wait days before you drive away your car? Here stands the competitive edge of the business – doing things better and faster than anyone else.

Highlighted here is the very clear relationship between organizational improvement and concrete business results – a link that many companies find hard to establish between culture change and the bottom line.

THE CHANGE ACCELERATION PROCESS – A CORE METHODOLOGY

You need to understand the background and the GE vision to understand the methodology of Accelerated Change. Many companies have emulated GE by committing to designing a variant of Accelerated Change. This evolved from Work-out and was part of a drive to do everything faster, better and cheaper. The belief was that most successful businesses are those that are able to respond quickly to changes and opportunities in their market. These are the ones that are excellent at getting new products to market, which can out-deliver the competition and generally do things better and quicker. Welch and his top team were driven by the belief that 'speed and responsiveness' could make you number one or two in any industry in which you operated. They used Work-out and Change Acceleration as core methodologies to give them a strong competitive advantage across the whole of their business empire.

APPLY THE SAME CHANGE METHODOLOGY TO ACQUISITIONS

It is GE's approach to change mastery that has delivered its competitive edge. Consider GE's progress. In the last 15 years GE has followed an enviable approach of acquiring attractive businesses and disposing of non-performers. On average, every day of the year GE acquires a new business. After the acquisition takes place and 'all the papers are signed' then it is up to the management team to integrate the new business into the GE culture through their post-acquisition integration strategies. It is vital to create a new entity that fits with the culture of the larger company. GE's approach to acquisitions is very similar to their methodologies in driving change.

GE has used 'time compression' in a special way, implementing change faster than anyone else. Doing things faster and better is now a core competency for GE. So what can we learn from this approach?

We can learn much from GE's focus on Change Acceleration, which was the summation of contemporary best practice in change management. The leading minds in 'Organizational Change' were challenged to develop models and tools that would promote the effective and speedy implementation of change. The result was the 'Change Acceleration Process' or CAP, devised through GE's Crotonville Business School in conjunction with their consultants. This continues to be an umbrella of organizational best practice focused on a seven-stage methodology, each stage relying on specific change tools and techniques. CAP worked. It focused on implementation not theory. It focused on action not talk.

Applying and tailoring CAP and other models within several GE businesses, my colleagues and I soon came to understand that some actions generated results faster than others. From this evolved our approach to change implementation, 'Rapid Improvement' (RI), which is based on our experiences and the tools of organizational development.

THE FIVE-STAGE RAPID IMPROVEMENT STRATEGY

These five discrete stages, with associated activities, take place in sequence. The stages are also process flows of actions created between the client and the internal and external consultant. The stages overlap one another and the actions inherent in each stage impact on each other. Whilst engaging in the first activity one must have given some consideration to developing the second, third, fourth and fifth stage. As explained in Chapter 1, change is a systemic process. As we introduce change in a 'cultural and behavioural' system or organization we cannot account for all the activities that arise from a particular action. We therefore need to seek continual feedback and adapt as we see fit. This reflects activity in the real world; the metaphor I use to illustrate its credibility is the 'airplane' analogy. All airplanes are only 'on course' for a few minutes of their total flight – no matter how long the journey – which is during take-off and landing. The rest of the time feedback from instruments helps the pilot or 'on-board self-correcting systems' to make minor changes to the flight trajectory.

PAYING ATTENTION TO FEEDBACK IS WHAT MAKES CHANGE WORK

Paying attention to feedback is the key issue in implementing change. Without feedback we do not know if we are on course or not. Failing to understand and access relevant feedback means that we have no means of knowing whether we are nearer to, or further away from, our goal. And although feedback is critical in letting us fine tune our trajectory for change, little resource and energy is devoted to capturing information that indicates the extent to which we have made specific, tangible progress. For example, we can launch a drive for change and run a series of public presentations outlining the purpose of the programme and yet fail to assess the response to it. Many people still have difficulty evaluating the effectiveness of even the most basic training course or workshop.

WHAT TO MEASURE – CULTURE AND RESULTS

The average organization fails to create the relevant metrics to use feedback constructively. There is an inability to document just how results are achieved. We fail to understand precisely what elements of the culture can be manipulated to create a specific goal. We have not traced a sequence of cause-effect relationships between our 'cultural and behavioural' inputs and our 'business' outputs. The real secret is to develop a scorecard approach[5] between the vision we have for the business and the indices, or performance measures, which tell us whether we are on course or not. It is possible to highlight specific 'behavioural' practices and actions that will yield specific results. Too few practitioners understand how to build this process into their organization. This is a major competency gap for internal consultants. They need to understand not only quantitative but also *qualitative* means of measuring culture and behaviour change. They need to be able to focus on the critical incidents that indicate whether a change has been accepted or not, or whether a new process is working. They need to develop behavioural tools to elicit the feedback that tells us whether we are making progress.

This continual quest for the interpretation of feedback is extremely powerful in assessing potential problems and error prevention; it is an important credo for anyone engaged in bringing about large-scale organizational change.

ASSUMPTIONS ABOUT OUR MODEL OF RAPID IMPROVEMENT

In order to understand the process of change we have to consider change as a sequence of events and, at the same time, as a flow of energies and activities. We have to be adept at ensuring that change is composed of a technical element and a cultural element. The technical element – a new system, structure or process that is to be installed – is taken for granted. How people respond to this technical change is what we need to address. This is where most change management methodology falls down. The five-stage approach is outlined below.

STAGE 1 – LEADING CHANGE

Change often fails because it is not led with passion and conviction. Sometimes change is not led at all! Often people do not commit to change because they fail to see a firm commitment from key players to the change. Because the major players in the business consciously fail to display enthusiasm for the change, people will tend to adopt a 'fence-sitting' mentality. For these reasons I firmly believe that 'Without leadership there is no change'. The people who sponsor a project or 'change' need to display behaviours indicative of their full emotional support for that change. The 'client' really needs to exude enthusiasm for the project. If the client cannot get excited about the project, why should anyone else? This enthusiasm has to be matched by the internal consultant, who must express the same energy, commitment and motivation for working with the client. This should be widely acknowledged whenever the project is discussed, especially in public.

Summoning up a high degree of 'emotional energy' to support a project is something that the client and consultant need to work on together. This does not mean being committed to printing special T-shirts or coffee mugs emblazoned with the latest initiative; it means giving careful consideration to the internal strategy of communication that will precede the change itself. The effectiveness of change can be greatly increased if the message of the change is well established in people's minds before they formally receive any training or development. There should be no confusion in their mind as to the actual need and rationale for the change.

During this phase the client and consultant should realize that any plan they develop cannot be written in stone. Systemic change involves a degree of flexibility to adapt to changes as they occur. This does not mean that things will go wrong. Indeed, it could mean a positive improvement, something happening faster than anticipated, for example. Flexibility is what makes change implementation work. We need this degree of adaptability to incorporate the 'feedback' discussed previously.

Does being spontaneous and flexible mean that there is no need for an implementation plan? Of course not; we do need a plan to indicate the key actions and milestones against deliverables. One great way to plan – taking into account possible adaptations – is to start with the end in mind.

DRIVING THROUGH THE REAR-VIEW MIRROR

Try this short exercise. Look into the future; imagine that a particular 'change' has been implemented. Now, placing yourself in this future, look back at events. Think about the plan.

- What worked and what didn't?
- What additional actions were required?

- If you had the time again, what would you have done differently?
- What were the real barriers to change and what could have increased the credibility of what you did, both as the consultant and the client in this process?

Looking back from an imagined future is like 'driving through the rear-view mirror'; it can present a completely different view of the plan of operations. Because you are now so close to the plan, distancing yourself using this technique is an interesting way of assessing what did and did not work.

Needless to say, any plan should be fairly detailed when describing the scope of the change as well as potential barriers. Focusing upon potential barriers helps you consider any preventative action you can take to anticipate and overcome resistance. At this stage it is important to use 'constituents analysis', a technique to assess the core interests of the key constituents or stakeholders in the change. By considering other people's perspectives you can develop a plan to minimize conflict between all parties to the process.

At this stage it is important to list the 'desired outcome' for the project, for all constituents. By detailing the consequences of the change, staff can understand the rationale for committing resources to the initiative. It highlights what is to come and, more importantly, sets the outcomes clearly in people's minds. Clarifying expected outcomes can help win commitment to change and define the parameters of the project – what it will and will not do.

STAGE 2 – CREATING A DESIRE FOR CHANGE

I am constantly amazed by the number of times companies have launched an initiative without communicating their intentions to the workforce. This practice is one of the main reasons why change fails. Before launching a quality improvement, customer focus or cost reduction exercise, organizations should think through the benefits of informing staff *in advance* of any roll-out. People should not be summoned to a training workshop or corporate launch of a new initiative without understanding why the change is necessary, and the tangible benefits that will accrue to the organization when the change is implemented. They also need to understand the roles and responsibilities they may need to adopt to support the initiative.

A cynic would say that what happens in practice is that several people get enthusiastic about a project; they know intuitively that it is the right thing to do. However, they fail to map all the benefits of a course of action. Then, because of their own impatience and failure to bring everyone on board, they launch their ideas and the project far too early.

What happens? The project fails. Their initial enthusiasm was not enough. They blame others for lack of foresight and vision. They blame others for resisting change. They don't give themselves the opportunity to think through the corporate and personal implications of the change. There was no direction, no plan – no roadmap or means of measuring progress. They failed to lead by example, and too much thinking was still in their heads. They had not tested for understanding or won the support of others. They failed to create a positive vision for the change and probably wasted a lot of resources.

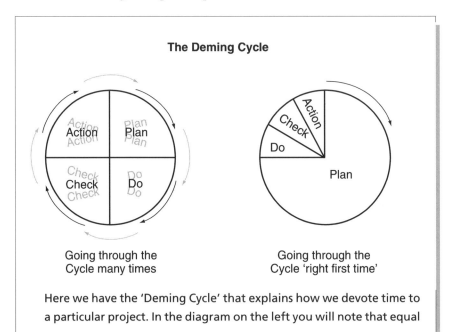

The Deming Cycle

Going through the
Cycle many times

Going through the
Cycle 'right first time'

Here we have the 'Deming Cycle' that explains how we devote time to a particular project. In the diagram on the left you will note that equal time is given to each of the activities – Planning, Doing (experimenting etc), Checking (inspecting and fine tuning) and Action (actually 'going live' with the project). Generally speaking, because of impatience, inattention to detail and working with the 'big picture' only, we devote insufficient time to Planning – thus creating a series of cycles reworking the whole sequence of steps several times; this lack of planning means the cycle has to be repeated over and over.

Now compare the diagram on the right to that on the left. We only have to go through the Deming Cycle once because we ironed out all the key issues during the Planning stage. By investing in prevention most problems can be foreseen and resolved before they occur.

The role of change leadership is to inspire people to commit their own time to organizational improvement. People need to be aware that the change is in the best interests of the company.

SELL THE SIZZLE NOT THE SAUSAGE

Change managers can learn a great deal from good sales people. Sales people will say that, when trying to persuade people to buy in to a product or service, the last thing you do is describe its features at length or in depth – that's boring. Sales people will say that you have to excite the customer about what the product can do for them, how it will make them feel. You are selling the 'benefits' that will accrue to them experiencing or possessing that product or service. Learn how to sell the sizzle not the sausage.

When devising any communications strategy a good start (used by any sales professional) is to assess likely objections to your communication in advance of its delivery. Compile a list of objections to the changes you are trying to implement and then develop a counter-argument for each one. Turn these into positive benefits that will evolve from commitment to the programme. That is the process of creating an effective communications strategy.

Beware of focusing too much on communicating the 'features' rather than the 'benefits'. The features by themselves are not especially compelling. They include core activities such as launch dates, the timing and content of any training workshops, the role of various players and the sequence of events categorizing the drive – the metrics of how change will be measured. Instead, sell the benefits that the business will accrue and paint a picture of how things will be better in the future. Remember to charge the benefits with positive feelings of emotional intensity. 'What will you feel after the changes have been implemented?' 'How will it change your world?'

Change agents and their clients need to remember that all they are doing is publicizing a programme; fundamentally, it is a major selling exercise! People will only accept change as legitimate if its rationale – and any resulting benefits – are clearly explained. We can learn much from sales people. Effective sales people focus upon likely objections that buyers will have to a proposal and counter these in their presentations. 'Objection Handling' is a very powerful process for selling a new initiative. Work out in advance likely objections and develop credible responses; then deliver these with enthusiasm and gusto.

Communication is key to effective change. Some companies devote huge amounts of managerial time to talking; but the quality of communication must be measured by what people receive, not what is sent. Stimulating a deep curiosity for the change, and selling the benefits, needs to be done at every opportunity. The 'communication' should create a compelling vision of what is to come, and should motivate people towards that future. Shaping a vision that people can work towards is a core activity, and it is not just the responsibility of the senior team. It is only through the interaction of all those involved in a structured process that specific visions can be defined.

STAGE 3 – ALIGNING CONSTITUENCIES

You need to make sure that everyone involved in, or affected by, the change is aware of who does what, when, where and how. This requires a plan of action with specific measures, time-frames and milestones. By examining how stakeholders and constituencies interact it is possible to smooth the transition and prepare for objections in advance. It is important to work out the specific motivations and degrees of co-operation between the various constituents or stakeholders. It is important to work through the core constituents; these would include your staff, staff representative groups, customers and user groups, suppliers, pressure groups, regulatory bodies and the media.

A communications strategy should be in place and should be regularly supported and updated to appeal to the interest of the core constituents. A 'one size fits all' communications strategy and message does not work. Each interest group or constituent will have different needs and priorities and may require specialist input on occasion. Orchestrating and aligning these constituencies is key to making change work. At this stage you need to mobilize all available resources to make sure that the vision each stakeholder or constituent will formulate is consistent with the vision of others. This is a massive communications exercise, often not practised by people from the 'rational-technical' school of change management. Here we are focusing attention on a vision of what the business is to become; we should recognize the style or mindset and behaviours that are reflected in that vision.

THE ELEVATOR SPEECH

Critical to any change initiative is the design of a simple yet compelling vision. This is essential if you want the people driving the project to clarify and articulate the vision of what is to result, in a simple and meaningful way.

An 'elevator speech' is a short 60-second message conveying exactly what you are trying to achieve. It gets its name from the chance meeting in an elevator with a newcomer to the business who knows nothing about your initiative. You travel three floors together and have just 60 seconds to convey your message. Knowing this, what would you say? Practise a speech outlining the rationale for change, the benefits of the process and the desired outcome for the business. If you do this you can reduce resistance to change.

Aligning commitment means gaining the support of the core actors, constituents or stakeholders affected by the change. Not everyone will be on your side all the time. We have to establish a critical mass of support and at the same time treat each of the constituents as individual groups with specific interests, needs and priorities. We have to address these differing needs and at the same time ensure that the core message is not diluted or the direction misaligned. What we are attempting to do is win support to our overall vision and goals. At the same time we are also identifying any possible resistance and, finally, making every effort to persuade, cajole and negotiate as required, to educate and inform. At every stage in the Rapid Improvement process we have to engage the interest and motivations of others.

STAGE 4 – SHAPING AN IMPLEMENTATION PLAN

Change is too often introduced without being project managed. There is too much focus on the training workshops or the application of tools rather than the overall implementation and installation of the project. People need to know where they and their team fit in to the process. They need to know the leverage points for change and how one factor influences another, and they need to know just as much about the benefits of the change as the features of what is to happen.

Change should be a strategic process that is managed from the top; too often, however, the management of change is more by accident than design. We need to create and practise a solid methodology so people can see where they are going (and understand the disadvantages of staying in the same place), comprehend the direction the business is pursuing and have a clear understanding of when the future desired state will be achieved.

This is the stage at which all the major drives for improvement are activated. It is often the time when training workshops are initiated, major launches are held to promote a particular activity, problem-solving groups are trained and the drive for Continuous Improvement really begins. We are starting out on a journey. We have planned sufficiently. We have led the project. We have developed a credible and persuasive communications strategy and cascaded it down to all constituents. We have identified where resistance may occur and taken action to win doubters over to our way of thinking. Only when we have completed these vital actions in Stages 1–3 can we really focus upon this period of learning, education and development. Organizations sometimes fail to commit to the first three stages and simply launch themselves headlong into training. The result is predictable; there is some heightening of activity and interest in a new initiative, but because it has not been well planned it soon becomes 'flavour of the month', yet another change initiative that failed, another fad that didn't work!

STAGE 5 – SUSTAINING CHANGE AND RELENTLESS IMPROVEMENT

Most change initiatives fail to achieve the synergies for which they were originally created. This is because we fail to plan for change within the wider political-behavioural context. Change is not a rational-technical process.

Experience shows that, for change to work, it has to be sustained and supported by key people in the business. It is not enough to launch the change initiative and believe it will cascade down of its own accord. Effective change needs to be fueled by enthusiastic people, people who feed back stories of how the change has benefited the organization.

Change is not a single inoculation to the system. It should be a transfusion of positive energy, injecting new blood at the right time into those areas of the business that need revitalization. Bear in mind that while you are feeding one particular initiative other projects may also be competing for attention and scarce resources. Sustaining a drive will determine the effectiveness of the initiative, and will tell you how well you managed to institutionalize the change into the organization so it becomes 'business as usual'.

Our overall goal is continuously to reinforce the message of the benefits of the programme in a very visible and tangible manner. The change has to be integrated into the evolving culture of the business. There will be many examples of processes that will require redesign to take account of improvements in ways of working.

CHANGE EFFECTIVENESS – METHODS AND KEY ACTIVITIES

Methods to Sustain Change	Key Activities
Leadership	Lead by example Make the change team core leaders Develop a model of leadership focused on change
Commitment	Be visible and support all activities Take action first Visibly commit top team players to presenting their support
Passion and enthusiasm	Energize self before energizing others Use every opportunity to talk about the change Give motivational talks
Communication	You cannot over-communicate Communication is what is 'received' not what is sent Seek feedback on what people have received
Early successes	Document and present success stories Spread best practice to all corners of the organization

Lessons learned	Be open about failures Demonstrate how learning improved the culture Create new training opportunities to reinforce the new culture
Recognition and reinforcement	Consistently reward desired behaviours Always recognize effort expended Create performance improvement linked to change implementation
Teamwork	Encourage people to work cross-functionally – most problems lie in processes between functions Use 'change' for team building; promote individuals based on their team skills
Resource allocation	Invest in areas where change is delivered Let budgets follow effort and energy Demonstrate that everyone is expected to achieve more
Quantifying progress	Establish cause-effect relationships, especially between a change in culture leading to business results Develop metrics and feedback Listen to what people think and feel about the change

It is vital that people understand the tools, processes and techniques for leveraging change; it is important to have a common core of knowledge about techniques that can be applied and documented.

The final area with 'Sustaining Change' is measuring, monitoring and quantifying progress. It is important to quantify the change in the culture because most people find it difficult to establish a clear link between business improvement and a change in culture. Culture change is not about 'tree hugging', it is about establishing strict causal relationships between the culture of the business and performance. We should be able to quantify the relationship between business process improvement and bottom line results, or equate effective teamwork with customer retention or the acquisition of new training skills with winning new customers. If we fail to form cause-effect relationships why should anyone commit to the change?

Monitoring change should reflect key mile-stones and build further commitment and momentum for the future. We need continually to strive to monitor and quantify progress. If we train, educate and observe changes in behaviour then we can reward those behaviours.

These changes themselves will at some stage result in a realignment of the infrastructure of the business and its methods of working. Finally, we don't just need to develop the ability to change but also the capacity to change. Our overall vision is to build this capability into the infrastructure and culture of the business.

Rapid Improvement Strategy

Leading Change

Creating a Desire
for Change

Aligning
Constituencies

Shaping an
Implementation Plan

Sustaining Change
and Relentless
Improvement

HOW THE FIVE-STAGE RAPID IMPROVEMENT STRATEGY WORKS

As previously stated, the process of Rapid Improvement deals with five stages, which overlap one another (see diagram). As we are working on Stage 1, Leading Change, we have to consider the other four stages simultaneously. For example, how will defining and scoping out the change initiative impact on the core activities in Stage 4 – 'Shaping an Implementation Plan'? Perhaps we need to involve other stakeholders in defining the precise nature of the project and seek clarification on our vision from their perspective? There are many such issues that need to be considered and integrated before the roll-out of change begins. It goes without saying that this is the core responsibility of the consultant and client, working together as a change team.

INTERNAL DELIVERY SYSTEM

There is little point devising a vision for the business if the organization does not have the in-house expertise to install and continually refine the process. Relying on external change agents for improving and installing change doesn't make sense for the average organization. It is vital to focus on moving managers beyond their technical or functional competence in order to create a group of people who are as skilled in the practice of change as they are in the application of their technical specialism.

This strategy of developing a team of high calibre change agents is unfamiliar to many businesses. Although most will at least commit to training their people in their core specialism, or the novel application of their basic skills, few will commit to training a selection of their managerial staff in the skills of change leadership. Yet the benefits are obvious. Once managers are skilled in change management their expertise can be called upon at any time to implement change, whether it is Customer Responsiveness, Re-engineering, Customer-focused Teams, Supplier Quality Assurance, Statistical Process Control, Quality Management, Material Resource Planning or installing a Just-In-Time philosophy! By equipping managers with the tools, techniques and processes underpinning successful organizational change the organization is developing a strong core competence, which can be relied upon for continuous renewal in the future. Training people beyond their technical function is clearly in the interest of most organizations, and yet few practise it.

Managers should be measured on achieving results through others. In reality, most managers are remunerated not for their technical knowledge but for their ability to get others within their team or group to achieve results. This is the real role of the manager; but how often do you encounter people who are not skilled in this area and who devote their time to the technical nature of their job, to the detriment of management and leadership?

WHO UNDERSTANDS THE PROCESS OF ORGANIZATIONAL CHANGE?

In my experience most executives and managers do not fully understand the dynamics of change, either in terms of how it relates to organizations or to individuals. Organizations need to develop a model of change that *works for them*, and then rigorously train their people in its application. Managers and leaders need to apply a consistent change management approach to avoid incoherence, chaos and confusion.

RESISTANCE IS TO BE EXPECTED

The reality is – most people don't like change. Probably the only people who do like change are those driving it! They are in the best situation to manage and lead any change because they know the purpose of the change, and its potential benefits. They may well have been involved in developing the change strategy, and so have a better chance of 'owning' the process than those who have never been consulted or involved in the process. Because they have devised the initiative they do not fear it!

It is easy to appreciate why people resist change if they don't understand why it is necessary. It is not surprising that most 'implementers' – the targets for change – don't commit immediately to 100% ownership. Often these people are classed as change resistors, and branded unfairly as such.

Understanding why people resist change may help you to structure a realistic model of action steps. In our consultancy work my colleagues and

I have concluded that we can implement changes quickly by following a definitive five-stage Rapid Improvement methodology. We are not suggesting that this is a perfect method and will suit everybody, but if you progress through these five stages you will probably avoid the major pitfalls that prevent successful change.

Change fails because:

- Leaders do not commit and take ownership; they fail to create a vigorous, energized vision of what is 'desired'.
- The client and the consultant have only a vague idea of the change they desire and don't define it in tangible, measurable terms.
- The changes are not described in sufficient detail to highlight how the 'present' culture can be transformed into the 'desired' culture.
- If there is a failure to lead once changes have been introduced, the organization has failed to develop a process or methodology to install the change and, more importantly, sustain it.
- The benefits of the change are often not explained, either from the corporate or personal standpoint. Short-term benefits and costs are often not explained in terms of what will happen to the business if change is not implemented.
- 'Communication is what is received, not what is sent'. This implies a real responsibility on senior managers to communicate effectively the benefits and expected outcomes of the change.
- The process of change (and the sequence of steps to achieve it) may be explained, but the benefits of pursuing change are not explored.
- Mobilize and align all constituents to the process of change. Analyzing how people may respond allows you to develop new strategies of influence that will project the intention more effectively. There may be many different constituencies who will be involved in the process, but don't expect them all to have the same needs and wants, each will differ markedly. So, design your communications strategy to deal with the differences which make the difference rather than relying on a generalized communication to be presented to all.
- Develop measures for performance improvement and make sure that

what is important to your change programme gets measured. Change fails when the initiative is not regularly reviewed. Audits by key people responsible for assessing progress and suggesting corrective or preventative action are simply not completed.

- Finally, because of what we call 'fad surfing', there is often no clearly understood process of Continuous Improvement that can be applied organization-wide. Often, a number of management fads are percolating through the business at any one time, with no over-riding theme clearly associated with driving the change process. Applying different methodologies at different levels and in different functions only confuses people and leads to further cynicism about the process of transformation.

CHANGE AGENT AND KEY PLAYERS

The process of change needs to be managed. Later, in Chapters 5, 6 and 7, I will highlight tools to help influence key actors in the process. The key actors are:

- those who are responsible for initiating, overseeing and leading the need for change – the clients (though all too often the clients don't see the need to lead the process)
- those who operationalize and drive the change – the internal consultants
- those targeted to implement change and who work with the consultants – the implementers.

Overall, it is the role of the consultant to work closely with the implementers so that they come to value the changes and take action to install them in their area of work. Chapter 4 deals with some potentially sensitive issues around consultants, clients and implementers working together as a core team.

SUMMARY

Mastering the change process has to be high on the agenda of most businesses. Developing a methodology is not something to which many businesses have committed, and yet it is critical that people can clearly see the rationale for the process of change and appreciate the benefits that the business will accrue. The methodology should be capable of dealing with 'rational-technical' as well as 'behavioural-political' issues. We can learn from other companies and institute best practice. Focusing upon the 'change team' is also fairly crucial.

- Change is a process with discrete stages and activities on which client, consultant and implementer can work together as a team. This is the challenge.
- To resist change is natural; people tend to prefer to stay within their comfort zones. People are usually busy and, however well the message that 'change is here' is conveyed, it will always be perceived as 'even more work'. It is unlikely that people will welcome change with open arms. It is important to win the support of those affected to any change.
- Understand that people may resist, rather than welcome, change as their first reaction; it is time to commit to a communications strategy that will sell the benefits of the change. Far too much time is devoted to the features or 'what will happen and when' rather than 'why'. Focus on selling the benefits rather than the features of change.
- Understand the causes of resistance to change and address these as objections before communicating the way ahead.
- Understand the reasons why change fails to be sustained, then understand why people do demonstrate cynicism.
- Use the five-stage Rapid Improvement model to think through the core activities that must be undertaken for success to be achieved.
- By examining the five-stage Rapid Improvement model you will soon realize that it is based on a 'prevention' culture. So, rather than dealing with problems as they arise, the prevention model 'front loads' activities to ensure that rework and errors don't occur.
- Finally, recognize that it is your role to make change a benefit to everybody involved, rather than a chore to be endured.

The Change Team –
The Role of the Internal
Consultant and Client

The success of any change initiative will depend not only upon a clear methodology or roadmap for change, but also upon the relationships that exist within the change team. The change team can be composed of a variety of people, but for simplicity's sake let's assume that we have a 'client' and an 'internal consultant'. In many cases we will also have an external consultant. Their input can be vital; they have a special edge due to their experience of implementing similar approaches (perhaps within the same industry). Occasionally, an external consultant is needed to say those uncomfortable things that make the client sit up and pay attention. At other times the external occupies no more than a technical role to get a project initiated and moving.

CRITICAL ISSUES IN THE CONSULTING RELATIONSHIP

Various issues arise when those involved in the process of change have to interact. There are many actors in the change arena, principal among these is the 'client', who has ownership of the project. As an internal consultant, your target audience is the 'implementers'. The consultant is charged with persuading, influencing and 'activating' the implementers to take the ideas, concepts, tools and processes on board, and implement them throughout the organization. The term 'implementer' has been chosen because it best sums up what the consultant is expected to achieve – the 'activation' of energy and the transference of ownership to implement change. Some people refer to these implementers as 'targets'[7] but this terminology implies that they have a passive part to play and are instructed what to do. I prefer the implementer description because it is more positive, empowering and suggests that those taking on this role have a strong, participative part to play rather than just being the subject – the target – for change.

I would like to keep the key people in the change arena discrete to these players, but in reality others are involved, including HR professionals and the management team. Consider the agenda of these people; review the relative health of the politics in the organization, particularly in the wider change team. Is everyone focused on the same deliverables? Does what you are doing conflict with the priorities of other change initiatives? What are the gains and losses for the change team if it does or does not work? Understanding these issues can have a significant effect on the outcome, and the decisions to which the change team will commit.

ORCHESTRATING ROLES

A key challenge when implementing change is the timely and seamless orchestration of events amongst the change team to ensure that the five stages of the Rapid Improvement model (Chapter 3) are fully actualized. The consultant must ensure that they really do win the commitment of the client to support the drive and open any necessary doors as things progress. Without this support consultants can only rely upon their own skills and abilities to influence and persuade others – we explore some key diagnostic tools relating to interpersonal relations in Chapters 5 and 6. It is critical to examine the relationships that exist within the change team, in particular the relationship between the client and the consultant. We need to identify and highlight the areas and issues where the client and consultant need to work together to make things happen.

THE RELATIONSHIP BETWEEN THE CLIENT AND CONSULTANT

The relationship between the client and the consultant (internal or external) should be that of 'one team' strongly driving change. However, in the real world there is sometimes disharmony between the consultant and the client; this is due to lack of understanding about how each believes 'change' should be progressed. There is ambiguity around each other's expectations. Sometimes the client and consultant simply haven't spent enough time defining requirements and both parties have failed to establish rapport towards the project. Both parties should always agree the purpose for – and the desired outcomes of – their respective roles.

ALIGNING EXPECTATIONS

It is useful to clarify the competing agendas of people within the change team. Everyone has their own, individual agenda. Below is a powerful process for working through the detail. It clearly establishes expectations between the internal and any external consultant and the client. It helps to manage expectations and is just as useful for examining a variety of external to internal relationships or internal customer to supplier relationships. It is about identifying and agreeing the expectations of both parties and managing any disagreement. The power of this instrument is that it requires answers to some really important questions.

MANAGING EXPECTATIONS

Each individual member of the change team should answer the following questions:

- What are the three core and specific deliverables that the change initiative will create for the organization?
- Define your specific role and the contribution you will personally commit to.
- What three personal goals do you want to come from this initiative?
- Where are the potential barriers to meeting the deliverables?
- What action will you take to prevent these barriers becoming no more than a nuisance?

> The change team needs to discuss specific responses and identify potential conflicts within the team, thus ensuring that all political and 'nuisance' factor issues are discussed before the project begins.

WHO IS THE CLIENT?

There are many interesting issues to emerge from this process, not least of which is 'Who is the client?' Sometimes the client is the person owning a problem, issue or change initiative. Clearly, ownership resides with one person, who may also be functionally responsible for a process. It is more difficult when there is joint or collective ownership of a project because the client is hard to identify. This is especially true when a consultant is facilitating the work of a steering group or executive team. The consultant has to keep on top of this 'client' issue, otherwise there may be little progress. In such cases, the consultant has to become more structured and agree an action list for assessing project completion and activity against time-frames. The internal consultant has to be able, on occasion, to assert himself.

WHO ARE WE TARGETING TO ACTIVATE THE CHANGE?

Write down the requirements of everyone in the change process. Failure to do this can derail the project, even before the real work gets started.

This is understandable when there is intense pressure to do something to correct or improve a situation. Speed of implementation should be viewed across the total process, not just the initial speed to get started. Look upon the process as a lifetime investment cost versus an initial purchase price. How often have you watched a sporting event where one team starts with a flourish of high activity, apparently sweeping the opposition aside, only to find by the end of the game that the team tires, runs out of energy and loses the game? Something similar happens in the workplace; many initiatives start with a great fanfare from a senior manager only to wither on the vine because the full requirements were not identified. The total cycle of events should be considered. This is exactly the same with the process of managing change – all actions and actors in the process have to be considered as working together to achieve the greater goal.

Often clients believe that everyone is as committed as they are to the process. However, it is not usually the client who encounters resistance at first hand but the consultant, when they try to encourage people to implement the 'process' within their own function, operation or locality. If preparation is poor there is a danger that the consultant's contribution will not be valued. Sometimes a member of the client's team needs help, but fails to understand that the expertise and resources are already on hand. The client may not be able to cope with the situation and may not believe that the internal consultant has the competence to resolve the issue. This is a common scenario, and one from which many external consultants gain employment – at the expense of the 'internals'.

THE VALUE OF EXTERNAL CONSULTANTS

External consultants can play an important role in driving change. They may have a great deal of experience. Perhaps they have worked on similar projects and can short-circuit some of the common teething problems by dealing head on with any resistance to change and winning the commitment of senior management. It is important to consider in detail what external consultants will achieve before you take them on. Are you clear about the purpose for which they are being engaged, and what precisely they will deliver? For example, I know of an excellent large consultancy that diagnoses key problems with customer service in large financial services businesses. After undertaking the diagnostic work, and completing a comprehensive report with recommendations for change, they expressly state that they do not implement the solutions! The point is clearly made at the beginning of any new assignment. Here the client organization has to make a decision about exactly what it wants. How keen is the organization not just to diagnose problems but also to establish a methodology for bringing about change? Some organizations still prefer objective analysis by a third party but, increasingly, more are interested in actual implementation. It is worth noting that the organizations that simply seek an objective viewpoint, and are not focused upon implementation, are probably not very serious about change. They want to debate the problems, not address them.

THE DOCTOR ANALOGY

In some ways an external consultant performs the role of a medical doctor. He diagnoses organizational health issues and then works with the patient/ client to prevent the problem or illness recurring. Without doubt, consultants can shake up an organization, they can wake it up to the reality of the need to change. Often an external is needed as an expert resource in change management or to express unpalatable truths to senior managers. External consultants are not dependent upon the organization for their career and perhaps can express their views candidly; internal consultants, on the other hand, may be making a career-limiting decision if they start to take on the 'big guns' in the business. Clearly, externals can be valuable to organizations, but I believe that they add most value when they are part of the change team. Here they will work with the internal consultant and ensure that specialist input is available; more importantly, they can ensure that the material or approaches are tailored to the culture of the individual organization. Here we have a degree of symbiosis between the external and the internal consultant, which is highly valuable.

BENEFITS OF WORKING AS A TEAM

The relationship between the internal and external consultant can be very powerful. I have worked with many internal consultants and HR professionals and through our collaboration we have been able to share experiences that benefit all parties. For example, I have frequently introduced internal consultants to clients from other businesses and sometimes they have worked with these other companies and the client on a project placement to discover how others approach change and run their business. Two examples come to mind. One involved placing several internal consultants from a bank with the Royal Mail and *vice versa,* the other concerned a senior change professional from the financial services sector being placed within a leisure resort and theme park complex. The benefits gained were: a recognition that change is a process applicable to all businesses and that change could be mastered; the experience of witnessing how other organizations manage the process and the realization that this can help you master skills and avoid pitfalls. The relationship between the internal and external consultant can be enriched by moving beyond the strict agenda of the change initiative. If you have employed or worked with external consultants in the past, have you really taken advantage of their experience of working with other clients and their network? If not, this should be on your agenda next time. They are a resource that can help you to develop the internal capability for change.

THE VALUE OF INTERNAL CONSULTANTS

Although in recent years many organizations have developed an internal capacity to change, at some point most projects require an element of intervention; externals are often brought in to work in an interim management role. In some cases these externals are then enticed to stay with the company with the strict remit of developing a degree of competency in that area of work. For example, after working with a major finance company, three out of six 'Process Mapping' specialists brought in to help design new systems were gradually integrated into the structure of the business and tasked with re-inventing a management consultancy unit focused primarily on technical input. Another organization employed two sales trainers to develop a sales training package for the retail industry; these were later tasked with further developing general retail training for the whole business. More and more companies are committing to some form of expertise in change management, but often with a role that is very technical and specific to a single project.

The following are examples of people who would be classed as internal consultants:

● Change Management consultants
● Trainers and HR professionals/advisors

- Quality managers
- Customer Service managers
- Call Centre managers
- Engineering support
- IT specialists
- Process Mapping specialists/Management Service practitioners
- Re-engineering consultants
- EFQM practitioners.

Working with these people to institute change on a larger and wider scale may be a good first step towards building a strong group of internal consultants. If these people have fulfilled the role of external at some time they are likely to be fairly independent, capable of working by themselves without much supervision or support. This is an important trait for any consultancy assignment; the last thing an organization needs is internal consultants who have problems asserting themselves and their views.

The role of internal consultant tends to be a technical rather than a change management role. Pure change agents or consultants are rarely developed or recognized as a resource within a company. Such people would find their way into a department of Organization Development and would only be used for special projects. Also, having a group of people circulating throughout the business without any functional responsibility, or reporting to a business unit, is highly unusual. We work in an environment where we have to justify expenditure against projects, functions or business units; any expenditure has to be examined in terms of its potential return on investment. As we know, we 'change practitioners' are not always able to justify our existence by claiming to tangible business improvements.

BEWARE THE BULLY

At some point as a consultant you will surely come across the client who is a bully. Bullies are difficult to work with because they are driven almost entirely by their ego and a wish to regulate and control others.

These people are difficult to deal with and will go to extraordinary lengths to dominate others. Being non-assertive and agreeing to anything outside your control with these people is pure folly.

The way to work with them is to come to an agreement with yourself that you will always follow your own rules. The rules are simple. Negotiate at every meeting the specific detail to which you and your client will commit; never generalize. Be precise and deliver what you can control. If you cannot deliver, be prompt in explaining the circumstances. Never, ever wing it! Often you may find that the bully is unreasonable and leaves an open-ended commitment for you to deliver. Always agree on how you will be measured. Seek clarification. Phrases such as 'Does that mean you want me to...', 'Thanks for your viewpoint but it seems to conflict with the other manufacturing priority agreed earlier' or 'Please tell me how this affects our previous agreement' can be useful. The only way to work successfully with a bully is to practise your assertiveness skills.

It is unlikely that an organization would be prepared to have a function or department of change experts with only a floating role. What is more, the culture of the business may well discourage the formation of such a group whose role many would perceive as being analytical, evaluative and critical. External change agents have to be forthright; they need to be prepared to speak up, even if this makes them unpopular. These traits are no different for the internal consultant and this style has to fit with what is 'comfortable' for the organization, especially the senior team. Many researchers in Organization Development have identified what is called the 'power-dependent' client (see Chapter 7 for details of the 'Regulator', one of four influential types). Such people will tend to be forthright in manner and independent, speaking their mind and displaying some quick thinking. Some may even display signs of regulation, control and impatience. This simply means that consultants must learn how to handle a variety of people, but especially those who created and lived within a Power culture as described above.

CASE STUDY

YOU DON'T CHOOSE YOUR CLIENT – THEY CHOOSE YOU!

Working with a group of engineers in a manufacturing business in the north west of England I was progressing through our three module approach to change mastery ('Managing Resistance to Change', 'Influencing Others to Lead Change' and 'Implementing Creative Solutions'). After working with eight people on the programme for just half a day I was approached by one of the engineers who stated that one of his clients was too assertive, interrupted him constantly and was generally dismissive if he did not present his case with enthusiasm. I agreed that I would play my part in helping improve his skills. We restructured the rest of the day to teach people how to use assertiveness techniques with their clients. Most people agreed to practise these skills. Two weeks later I asked the individual how he had fared with his client. He told me that he had been too scared to use his new skills whereas the others had braved the slings and arrows and endured. The individual asked me whether there was any other way I could help. I had to be honest. Being a change agent or internal consultant requires a certain amount of self-belief and confidence. Failing to be more assertive, when required, creates stress, achieves little for the company and reinforces the client's behaviour as being acceptable. This was not what the engineer wanted to hear, but it was the truth. Anyone can be a consultant but they just have to commit to learning to improve their skills and take some risks.

Consultants have to learn to manage the client. This is an essential skill. Managing a client's expectations and aspirations has to be a top priority.

To be effective, the consultant must display a range of characteristics to deal with a variety of clients; these characteristics don't always fit senior managers' expectations of how a good consultant should behave. However, they may be precisely what is required. To be effective the consultant needs to be assertive, independent and speak up when they see that things are going wrong. However, this does not always go down well. In some business cultures senior managers prefer others to adopt a compliant role and fit in with the culture rather than challenge it. Personally, I believe we need people to speak their mind and certainly, in the General Electric culture described previously, this is the preferred way to do business. To be polite but challenge and improve on anything that stands in the way of progress has to be a prime consideration.

PERSONALITY AND CHARISMA

Personality is central to many of the roles required of the consultant. They need to display resilience and be prepared to speak their mind. Personality factors are important in shaping the behaviour that we expect consultants to display. The use of personality instruments such as 16PF, Myers Briggs, Firo-B, OPQ (Occupational Personality Questionnaire – Saville & Holdsworth) and others are important tools in helping consultants to assess their own personal styles and preferences, and how better to work with different people. Learning how to deal with various types of personalities is critical to achieving as much as possible from the change team. (More detail on this approach can be found in Chapter 8.)

Many of our programmes in developing 'Consultancy Skills' and 'Mastering the Politics of Change' concentrate on reading the personality preferences of other people more effectively. This quite simply helps us to manage the behavioural components in the change arena.

Examining the team profiles (in Chapter 8) you may find that some of the character types needed to promote change, such as the more assertive and abrasive 'Driver' and the ideas-orientated but introverted 'Innovator', are not always welcomed as team players. These people may be perceived more as 'team busters' than 'team builders' – but their inclusion in the change team is critical. 'Innovators' are few and far between within a company and are often regarded as mavericks or difficult people to work with. 'Innovators' are people who can look at things differently; a key asset in a change agent or consultant. I believe that consultants need to challenge the *status quo*, creating a 'wake-up call' to those in business to continually strive to re-invent the organization.

TRANSFORMERS VS TRANSACTORS

Originally developed from Warren Bennis' Transformational and Transactional Leadership patterns, we must focus on change being driven by two extreme types or approaches. This is a theme many businesses have had to assess for themselves, especially when looking for a dominant and change-orientated leadership role for their managers. Research would tell us that companies have encouraged the 'Transactional' type of manager to predominate over their counterpart, the 'Transformer'. The Transactional type is someone with a keen and detailed knowledge of a function, who is good at transacting business, who relies on analysis, is focused upon the short term, committed to ends rather than means and will use established business knowledge to fix things when they go wrong. It is difficult to question the contribution of these people. We rely on them to provide continuity.

Now consider the alternative style, the Transformer. This style is less predictable and these people can be difficult to manage. Again, this dominant management style will soon have a significant impact on the business culture. These people are referred to as 'transformational' managers who adopt a stronger and more assertive role, and who are committed to achieving results in the longer term.

CHANGE MANAGEMENT – TRANSFORMATIONAL AND TRANSACTIONAL LEADERSHIP

Transformational Change Leader	Transactional Change Leader
Visionary and inspirational in motivating others to achieve	Technically focused – good at analyzing solutions to complex problems
Strategic thinking, forward planning, focused on the future	Short-term orientated

Intuitive and creative – thinking 'outside the box'	Advanced analytical thinking – looking for the right answer
Active and energized	Passive and reactive to events
Change orientated	Maintaining stability
Challenging	Clarifying

Transformers may appear to be a little 'off the wall' in terms of their ideas and creativity. They are also much more difficult to manage than the Transactional manager and their approach can be a challenge for the top team member who prefers conformity and compliance to challenge and the pursuit of creative ideas. Transformational managers will 'think out of the box' and take action before considering the consequences. They will be impatient for success. Adopting a transformational role is critical if the organization has to change, and change quickly. But simply replacing the safer transactional with a transformational manager does not work. You need a combination of these two types – one group to transact, to deliver results, the other to transform the business. Ideally, you need a mixture of the two approaches in the same person, and that is probably the ideal role for the internal consultant – transformational in outlook but transactional in delivery.

Every organization must assess whether it has the right mix to ensure continuance while meeting the challenge of change. The organization needs to think about what kind of change agent they want to develop to shape their business for the future.

CASE STUDY

TRANSFORMATIONAL LEADERSHIP – THE DRINKS BUSINESS

This case study concerns an extremely successful European producer and distributor of fine wines and spirits. My consultancy's intervention began in the grain-distilling business that provides most of the spirit grain for a variety of brands. The intervention was to work with a newly formed top team, who renamed themselves the 'Leadership Team' because of the importance of leadership in the change process. The team had specific strategic objectives regarding the supply, and reduction of the cost, of raw materials to the business. The new team had several challenges; they decided to commit to transforming their existing business culture into one that was required to drive and lead change in the future. Their efforts, plus the energy of the 30 people who reported to them, were central to achieving both the required cultural and business results within the time-frame. Work continued into the Malting division and to other parts of the business. Various workshops were run for many levels of management throughout the business with the theme of 'Transformational Leadership'. During workshop sessions all participants worked on personality profiling, 360 degree assessment of leadership style, the application of Myers Briggs to team development, managing conflict, handling resistance to change and developing superior communications skills as well as acquiring the skills to manage the transition to the new culture.

Benefits

- A firm commitment was demonstrated to understand how the Leadership Team of the business could drive change. Through a series of leadership workshops the top team applied many change management tools (eg 360 degree appraisal, influencing strategies, team development activities and transactional analysis) to bring about the required change in management style.
- Leadership and living the values became a dominant aspect of the culture.
- Development centres were created to ensure that change leaders acquired the understanding and commitment to deliver competence in 'change mastery'.
- Much of the learning from this intervention has been continued in other divisions, with the leadership focus becoming the central driver to transforming business.

Once this decision is made it is quite simple to examine the key stages and issues to be managed by the consultant. They have to manage the client, the implementers and other constituents in the process – not an easy task if the consultant has only been trained in a technical specialism. As already mentioned, consultants must undertake a rigorous personal development programme to prepare themselves for this demanding role.

REAL-LIFE PROBLEMS WITH CLIENTS – HOW WOULD YOU DEAL WITH THESE ISSUES AS AN INTERNAL CONSULTANT?

Below is a selection of organizational problems. These problems are all real client issues that have existed in projects experienced by myself and my colleagues. Obviously, the responses need to be more detailed than outlined here but several influencing strategies will be employed (see Chapter 7). An important point to make is that the internal consultant is not entering a popularity contest; they should be aware of the need to assert themselves and take some risks.

Problem 1 – Clients do not know what they want, nor do they understand their role.
Response – The consultant may have to detail the whole change process for it to work. The best way forward is to agree to develop a 'role and responsibility' matrix detailing the core issues that need to be resolved in the whole project, using the five-stage Rapid Improvement model (Chapter 3).

Problem 2 – Clients do not want to be the 'client', taking ownership and responsibility for a project. Perhaps they have been coerced into becoming the client by their boss, CEO or others. They will do all they can to avoid responsibility and put the onus on the consultant to drive the change.
Response – Some clients try to evade responsibility for a variety of reasons. The consultant must take action to focus upon the positive

and active role the client should take. Highlighting the consequences of the project failing – and asking the following questions – may help:

'How are you being measured in this project?'

'What are the consequences for you if this does not work?'

'How would your colleagues react if the expected changes do not occur?'

Asking questions that highlight the probability of negative things happening – personally to the client – may be sufficient 'away from' motivation and leverage to get them to take action. The idea that 'sanctions' can be applied may encourage the client to take things seriously.

Problem 3 – Clients being chosen (by their boss or others) who are on their way out of the organization, have been sidelined or are due for early retirement because of poor performance.

Response – Real care has to be exercised here. Any resulting poor performance in your project may actually aid the client in speedily exiting the business, which may be to their liking! Focus on roles and responsibilities. Make every effort to discover who will replace the client should they leave the business. You need to make the existing client aware of your discomfort at having a potential change of client midstream; you should talk through the issue with their senior manager. When you do get access to the current client's senior manager, you may consider discussing issues of transferability of ownership once your existing client leaves the company.

Problem 4 – Clients do not believe in the project and are 'hosting' it because no one else will.

Response – Again, the client will try to get out of the responsibility, avoid it or blame you if it doesn't work. Work through the 'role and responsibility' exercise stated in Problem 1.

Problem 5 – Clients claim that you are the expert, and that they are too busy with other projects.

Response – Counter this by stating that without their support the whole project will fail. Their ability to 'open doors' and visibly support your actions will make all the difference. No amount of expert skill is going to get others to change, but perceiving the support of the client will change people's views.

Problem 6 – Clients who believe that the project has only a technical dimension and have no confidence in the behavioural approach to change, viewing it as no better than 'tree hugging'.

Response – This is a major problem and more widespread than most people think. It is important to understand that the career path and experience of the client will have done much to shape this attitude. It is only through tangible evidence that you can win the support of the client to the credibility of some of the tools and solutions you may wish to use. You have to focus only on those events that cause other results to improve. So, what action can you take to help the client associate changes in the culture and processes with definite performance improvement? What action can be taken in shaping behaviour to generate specific actions resulting in doing things faster, cheaper, better?

Problem 7 – The client is more than one person. It is difficult to win the tangible support of the whole client group. You meet with the client as a 'steering group' that seems to be little more than a 'talking shop'.

Response – You have to agree to a checklist of actions for the steering group and, against this, list names alongside responsibilities, time-frames, review periods and measures. You have to drive this approach at all times.

Problem 8 – The client agrees to take action but fails to do so.

Response – Agreement to an action plan must be forthcoming and you must state firmly that you cannot progress until the action is taken. You can also claim that progress will not be achieved in other areas until the relevant action is taken.

Problem 9 – The client uses the external consultant more than the internal consultant.

Response – You have to discover why there is more confidence in the external. Find out how the external is being measured. What attracts the client to the external rather than you? Make every attempt to work closely with the external, agreeing boundaries and overlaps.

Problem 10 – The client is a bully.

Response – Be assertive and agree ground-rules about how you will work with each other. Bullies only bully those who don't stand up to them. They pick on people who are compliant and have a lack of self-esteem. Bullies tend to pick up the low energy emitted by victims. Stand up for yourself; be brave. No matter how senior the client is, any attempt on their part to bully or use fear cannot be tolerated.

CORE ISSUES FOR THE INTERNAL CONSULTANT

As previously stated, the internal consultant orchestrates events, working closely with the other actors in the change arena. The change agent or consultant has some key issues to resolve; these are noted below.

PAY ATTENTION TO THE RIGHT ISSUES

The internal consultant must ensure that issues to be resolved or improved upon are clearly identified and defined in order to examine cause-effect relationships. They have to be able to know what causes things to happen and where to apply leverage. Issues related to the politics of change need to be aired with the client.

A key role of the internal consultant is to pay attention to the correct issues in terms of generating information upon which to base decisions. Traditionally, the focus has been on developing quantitative data but, increasingly, gathering qualitative data is considered paramount. Change is not only about trends and indices, it is about emotions, feelings and attitudes.

Identify the process flow of energy and those who drive the process – the core constituents of the process. The consultant must act as a facilitator and work with those who will profit, or lose, from the intervention. This implies that the consultant has to be an honest broker and be seen to be neutral. If the consultant has too much emotional energy tied in to a particular viewpoint, objectivity will be called into question.

> ## THE INTERNAL CONSULTANT:
>
> - Is an expert in change management.
> - Understands what makes people tick, and how to change behaviour.
> - Is politically adept and can manage conflict.
> - Can present unpopular viewpoints.
> - Influences and persuade others with integrity.
> - Is a trainer and an educator.
> - Designs learning experiences.
> - Facilitates discussion.
> - Coaches others towards improved performance.

The internal consultant must learn to work with, and manage, the relationship with the external consultant, even if the external is senior in rank and experience. The responsibility of the internal consultant is to achieve the best value from the external. When an external consultant is used they should be a very strong 'connector' between the client and the internal consultant. The role of the internal consultant is not to do the work – and take 100% ownership – that is the job of the client.

OWNERSHIP

Ownership for change rests with the client. The consultant is the facilitator to make change happen. The internal consultant may have ownership for the process delivering the change, but ownership for the project must lie with the client. The client has to feel that they are the driving force behind the project. It is up to the client to bring pressure to bear on any parts of the organization that do not want to change. The internal consultant must ensure that those within the organization do the work to enable the required change or improvement. The senior people must take ownership, through 'clientship' for the project, and install the necessary processes and procedures to ensure the success of the project. If there is no internal consultant to bridge the gap between the theory and practice, the external consultant can become frustrated because action is slow or non-existent. So, in order to get the best out of the external consultant, you need an equally strong internal consultant.

SUMMARY

Successful change management does not depend upon strict adherence to a methodology, no matter how sophisticated. Although the method, or roadmap, is important for guiding actions, the really important factor is managing relationships and expectations, and understanding the chemistry of the change team. This responsibility rests fairly and squarely with the internal consultant. It might entail being brave and taking a few risks, but this is the investment required to make change work. Committing to building a strong team is fantastic personal development.

- Internal consultants need to understand how to influence with integrity, with win-win solutions the goal.
- A core competency for any person occupying the role of consultant is the ability to be assertive, positive and optimistic.
- Success in the change team is determined by how well the aspirations and expectations of the team are juggled and agreed. The team must be orchestrated to play in tune, and the expectations of team members regularly reviewed.
- Be aware of political undercurrents, particularly with members of the change team who are only partially involved in your project.
- As a consultant you will encounter resistance in various forms from the people you meet in your sessions and workshops, and in the discussions you have with other people on the change team. Be alert to the fact that

your client may not recognize this; they will not be aware of any resistance unless you tell them.

- Identify the client; is it the person responsible for implementation, or the person who will be most hurt if the project does not succeed in its objectives?
- If you have a multiple client group, pay special attention to deliverables and action lists.
- Some clients may display the dominance, and even the characteristics, of a bully. Always be aware of how you can deal with bullies at an early stage. You will have to be brave and assert your viewpoint rather than be dominated.
- Remember that your client chooses you, not the other way around.
- You have to learn to manage your client and your boss.
- Personality and charisma are powerful allies in helping you manage the change team. You achieve more by influencing and persuading others than telling and directing them.
- Understand the basis of personality, and the key models that explain how to deal with personality differences.
- Ensure that 'ownership' rests with the right people.

Action Research –
The Consulting Cycle,
Psychological Contracting

Action Research[8] is a term that we use to focus attention on actively examining and analysing a problem, formulating a solution and then taking action. It is an excellent way to look at consultancy interventions and the stages through which they need to be progressed. In this chapter I will focus initially on a general approach to problem solving and then concentrate on the key activities in what has evolved into a way of working with all those in the change team – the 'Consulting Cycle'. This cycle of events concentrates upon core issues, activities and desired outcomes for each phase. This approach reflects the activities that require closure and are detailed in the Rapid Improvement methodology outlined in Chapter 3.

PREFERRED STYLE OF CONSULTING

An excellent introduction to problem solving within a consulting relationship is the approach outlined by Kolb.[9] This approach suggests that we each have preferences in methods of learning and solving problems that tend to be reinforced in our professional lives. As we develop a preference, for example, 'being practical and fixing things as they go wrong', we develop strength in that particular area. Gaining strength in one or two ways of learning and problem solving reinforces our belief about what style works best for us. There is a danger of becoming too specialized or always dealing with any issue or problem in exactly the same way. Because this approach worked in the past we are confident it will work in the future. However, in a consultancy role you need to be flexible and adapt your approach to the circumstances.

Kolb's Learning Styles

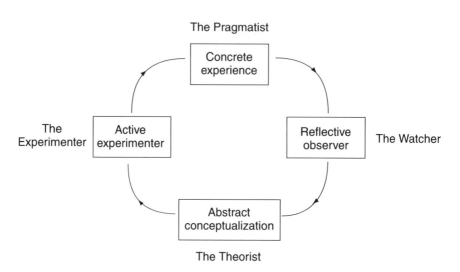

The Learning Styles approach can be a powerful way to get people to assess how their preferences for learning about, or solving, an issue can colour their judgement. Let's assume that consultants are very good at reacting to events. Let's say that they witness a particular problem – they have a 'concrete experience' (see diagram) of something not working as well as it could. If they adopt a similar style to the 'Pragmatist' they will metaphorically roll up their sleeves and deal with the problem then and there, working on it until it is resolved. This is a short-term and immediate solution. Kolb's approach would tell us that this is a fine way to respond, but if we persist in using this style, and always adopt the Pragmatist's approach, this may not be appropriate to resolve the larger problem in the longer term. Alternatively, Kolb would suggest that for real learning to take place consultants need to be more flexible. For example, if they witnessed a problem, instead of diving in and playing the role of the Pragmatist, they may wish to look at the problem from different angles before taking any more action. They could learn from the role of the 'Watcher', the reflective observer of events. The Watcher will collect data to assess the seriousness of the problem, reflect on that data and then form an opinion as to what went wrong. Then, if they adhere to the Kolb approach, they would move into 'Theorist' mode and conceptualize realistically about what caused the problem to manifest itself. They will then formulate a hypothesis and move to the next stage – 'Experimenter' – when they take action to resolve the problem based upon their theorizing, in turn based upon the quality of the data with which they have worked and the actual experience itself. This approach means that consultants can look at a problem from many perspectives, in this case as the Pragmatist then Watcher, Theorist and Experimenter. It doesn't matter where we start in the process, as long as the whole cycle is completed.

The benefit of this approach is that it offers a rounded perspective on examining and solving problems. It means that we should not just react and 'jump in' to resolve a problem. This is important if one or two of these 'learning styles' are the accepted and dominant approach to fixing problems in a business. In certain businesses the accepted style is that of the Pragmatist – fix it now, and at any cost! One organization in which I consulted adopted the dominant style of learning somewhere between Pragmatist and Experimenter. When something broke down in the production process all the managers immediately descended on the problem to try and fix things, using a variety of actions. It was a 'try this then try that' approach, with no thought to collecting data and working through a logical process. It was an approach based on pure gut reaction. There is a danger that this becomes the dominant company-wide learning or problem-solving style, based solely on 'fix-experiment, fix-experiment'. If this is the case there is little opportunity to use other approaches which may be more effective. This example is directly applicable to the consulting process. Is there a dominant or preferred way of doing things in your business? Does this style or approach always work? Does the organization use a 'hit and miss' approach? Does the business focus too much on analysis, reflection and theorizing and devote insufficient energy to action? Are there other approaches that may generate better results for the consulting team?

Overall, the Kolb approach is a good tool for furthering understanding of how problems have been addressed in the past. If you go back in time to examine the approaches an organization has applied to change you will undoubtedly find a dominant pattern emerging, a pattern which probably reflects the dominant management style of the person responsible for change implementation.

THE CONSULTING CYCLE

To avoid the straitjacket 'one best way' or 'preferred style' of problem solving, examine the Consulting Cycle (see p100). This is based upon the 'Action Research' approach and incorporates much of the thinking illustrated in the preceding pages. As we progress through each phase, reference will be made to key issues and desired outcomes for core activities.

PHASE 1 – ENTRY AND THE PSYCHOLOGICAL CONTRACT

There are several stages to the consulting process, which apply to both internal and external consultants. The first is the 'Entry and Contracting' process. At the start of the project the consultant should do all they can to create a positive 'psychological contract' with the client. Much has been written about the psychological contract and it is considered critical to the effective implementation of change. Unfortunately, in many consultancy interventions the psychological contract is an 'unconscious' agreement between the consultant and client, ie the two or more parties never openly discuss all the issues around making the change team most effective. Expectations are not voiced or debated (see the 'Expectations' exercise in Chapter 4), leading to the client and consultant forming unrealistic assumptions about how each should exercise their relative duties, obligations and activities, and the standards of behaviour by which the tangible elements of the project will be achieved. All too often the reason change does not succeed is because right from the start the client and consultant fail to agree the full extent and detail of how they will work together. The consultant must be prepared to discuss and educate the client as to the nature of any verbal agreement they have expressed as to how work will progress.

CASE STUDY

CONFUSION IN THE CONTRACTING PROCESS

A colleague was working as an external consultant in a large insurance business, driving through a major culture change initiative around customer focus both inside and outside the business.

This consultant worked closely with the internal consultant. Their relationship was amicable, but my colleague was concerned that the internal consultant had not negotiated a solid agreement with the client – the HR Director for the business. Although he was the client (given the job by the CEO), the HR Director was not really committed to seeing through all the necessary changes in his own functional area. He believed – wrongly – that the HR function had no emerging problems and that the issue of 'customer focus' was everybody else's problem, not his own. In reality, my colleague knew that the HR Director was not committed to the process, lacked self-criticism and just wanted to be seen to be doing the right things. The Director had not allowed his people to attend any training because 'that is their stock in trade and it is a waste of their time attending'. The key point here was that there was a non-verbalized and tacit agreement between the internal consultant and the client which was that under no circumstances would there be any debate or criticism about HR being involved in any training or development related to the intervention. The internal consultant knew it was a problem, and the HR Director knew that the internal consultant was aware of the problem, but the issue was never raised in discussion.

> My colleague, the external change agent, had to approach the issue differently and managed to achieve a shift in the director's attitude; however, this example illustrates the problems that arise due to a failure to discuss issues around what needs to be agreed 'psychologically'.

The psychological contract is not a formal agreement documented and signed in the same way as a service level agreement. It is, however, an understanding between the client and the consultant about how they will work together to achieve the objectives tied in with the project.

THE PSYCHOLOGICAL CONTRACT

The psychological contract is an agreement that binds all parties to agreed ways of working. A psychological contract usually involves:

- Objectives – general, specific and evolving as the project progresses.
- Review periods – their frequency, key milestones and associated activities.
- Metrics – precisely how will progress be assessed?
- Time expected to be devoted to the project – from beginning to end.
- Expected percentage of time devoted per week to the project – for example, is the project full-time or part-time and what percentage of the week is the consultant expected to work on the project?
- Confidentiality and secrecy agreements.
- Deliverables agreed by both parties.
- Use of external resources, such as change agents external to the organization.
- Agreement on how the internal and external consultant will work together.
- Training and development time for the internal consultant.

- Resources available.
- Budget constraints.
- Access to client.
- Standards of behaviour.
- Defined expectations.
- Means for resolving conflict.

It is a living agreement about how priorities will be achieved and the accepted standards of behaviour for working together. It is about developing a joint agreement to work together as a seamless team. As the relationship evolves so the contract will change. It is not – and never should be – a formal document stating precise responsibilities.

The establishment of a rapport between the client and consultant must be the first objective for both parties. Both must feel comfortable with one another. If there is more than one consultant or client involved then this will obviously take longer to accomplish. Time must be allowed to secure good rapport. The relationship must be solid and durable. If you are the internal consultant always identify the primary contacts – the primary or sole client and primary or sole external consultant. Establish what is to be delivered by both parties; this can prevent misunderstandings later on and ensure support for the project.

Critical to the process is gaining insight into the 'history' behind key problems. Consultants must collect information and data. They must try to identify plausible cause-effect relationships. Test for history; much can be learned from the past. Has a similar project ever been undertaken? Ask questions; are events recurrent? Has the issue been worked on previously with little or no success? This is something that requires particular attention and research; why did previous improvement attempts fail? Who worked on the issue before? Was it an internally or externally resourced project or task? Collect as many symptoms of the problem as possible; this can be very informative when trying to identify some of the root causes of the problem. It can also be useful in identifying the actual decision-makers within the client's organization. The consultant must agree with the client who they will be working with. Is it one or more people? If more than one, who is the primary contact? What is the credibility, experience and ability of those with whom the consultant will be working? How long have they been involved with the company, the situation? For how long will the resources be available to the consultant?

Before proceeding to the next stage, make sure that you have a contract, an agreement of what is involved in your role as the consultant and to what the client is actually committing. This contract is two-way. It is about relationships, it is about the trust and integrity of all parties. Any consultant should ensure that both they and the client are in agreement over each other's roles and responsibilities, including those of every other individual working on the project. Roles, responsibilities, desired outcomes, time-frames and resources must be clearly defined and confirmed between the two principal parties – the consultant and the client. When all of the above has been done, then proceed. Beware of future misunderstandings, conflict and abrasive relationships if the process underlying the psychological contract is not completed.

The Consulting Cycle

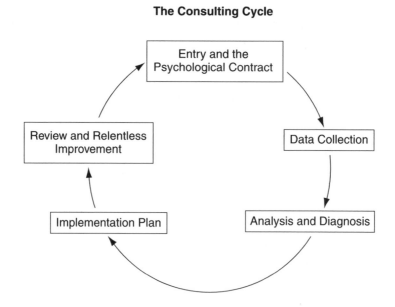

PHASE 2 – DATA COLLECTION

The second phase is Data Collection. This is akin to the role of the 'Watcher', when we objectively reflect on the situation from a third party perspective. The consultant should determine what data is to be collected, and from where. The consultant must not make assumptions about the state of readiness of the organization to change. What variety of data do you need to collect? Is it fundamentally a quantitative data-gathering activity? Do you have the tools and techniques to ensure that the data-gathering process is objective and fair? Can you design any requisite tools such as attitude surveys, leadership profiles, cultural reviews, customer service questionnaires? If you do not have this specialist expertise yourself, do you have access to someone who does?

Have you considered using qualitative means of data collection and analysis? If you use this approach, for example mystery shopping, scenario planning or focus groups, how can you ensure that the data will be 'clean' and that any discussion between the consultant and the interviewees is confidential? Can you ensure that focus group members will not discuss group input with others on their return to their specific function within the organization? Can you ensure that the senior people involved in this process will respect the need for caution in expressing their ideas to other audiences, after staff have contributed their ideas in group settings such as focus groups?

Is the data readily available? Over what time-frame will it be made available? Here the use of internal consultants can be invaluable; they know the organization better than the external consultant and can track down and extract data. You may find it useful to employ an additional 'internal resource', someone chosen for their interpersonal as well as technical skills, someone who can work full-time on data and information collection over a concentrated period of time.

Confidentiality and Trust

Do not work in a vacuum. People often resist change because they do not know the agenda you seek to deliver. Ensure, as far as possible, that you are open in your dealings. I regularly interview senior managers and find myself having to work hard to convince interviewees that anything they say to me is treated as confidential. This issue can sometimes create problems for the internal consultant, simply because they may not enjoy the same seniority as those they interview. And sometimes the consultant has to ensure that any sensitive strategic information disclosed to them remains totally confidential.

CASE STUDY

CONFIDENTIALITY CRISIS

When working on change interventions my colleagues and I focus on examining the 'change leadership' capability of senior managers. In this example a colleague, Edward, was the external consultant and the relationship with the client, Bob, evolved into one of formal coaching. The coaching focused upon Bob's core life options, his decisions in business and his relationships with others. Out of the blue, Edward received a phone call from Bob's boss, Peter. My colleague was told, in no uncertain terms, that he was required to attend a meeting with Peter and that he should be prepared to discuss Bob's progress. Edward politely stated that the nature of the coaching work was confidential with Bob and that he could not disclose any information, apart from the most general. Peter, well known for his dogmatic approach and focus on control, then demanded to meet Edward with the same request to talk in detail through Bob's development plan. At this point Edward felt he had to withdraw from the coaching work. In the meantime, Bob had been put under intense pressure by Peter to disclose the content of those discussions, which were extremely sensitive. There was no option but to 'walk away' from the intervention. Peter's curiosity and need for control was a major barrier to any development work Bob wanted personally to pursue.

The major learning point here is that there will be times when external consultants will be put under pressure to disclose information given to them in confidence. Consultants have to demonstrate integrity and adhere to their values. Be under no illusions, this reality permeates many organizations and the consultant needs to demonstrate some strength of character to maintain their integrity and confidentiality.

360 Degree Data and Feedback

Feedback is critical to creating strong and evolving change management plans. The quality of data and feedback is determined by the ability of the consultant to create a climate of mutual trust, where views from people throughout the organization can be incorporated to formulate a realistic diagnosis. This may mean attracting opinions from several levels and functions within the organization. As a consultant you need to ensure that, where necessary, you work with a cross-section of the organization, canvassing their views and therefore ensuring a rigorous and accurate diagnosis.

Obtain data and information from those who know facts and detail. Don't allow yourself to work with only a select few managers or supposed experts, this will deprive you of essential data and information crucial to your diagnosis of the problem.

Building Rapport

As an internal consultant the ability to build rapport is critical to developing trust with interviewees, the client and those with whom you will be working to execute changes – the 'implementers'. Later, in Chapter 7, we will be discussing the need to read the motivations of others with whom you are engaged. This requires a firm commitment to learning more about what drives behaviours and to becoming more psychologically aware and astute. As a consultant you need to make sure that you plan and execute this phase well. Take as much time as you and your client can comfortably accommodate. This is the foundation for your future recommendations.

PHASE 3 – ANALYSIS AND DIAGNOSIS

The third phase is Analysis and Diagnosis. What do the collected data tell you? Ensure that your data is triangulated, ie that you have several categories of data that will enable you to be confident in its reliability and any subsequent diagnosis. Ensure that you are measuring the right things (which are very specific to your intervention) and that your diagnosis is solid and verifiable. Be careful to stay within the client's brief. You will have generated a great deal of data and there is always the opportunity to pass comment on things beyond your remit. Ensure that you triangulate data from several sources or various methods or points in time. Examine the data from more than one angle; this helps test its accuracy and integrity.

Focus groups are powerful sources of qualitative data. Asking the right questions can yield a plethora of data, but sometimes there can be too much. You need to keep the focus group on time and ensure that their contribution is relevant to the issue under investigation. Whilst maintaining control, you have to be sensitive about how you treat people who are enthusiastic, but who tend to stray from the point. A highly focused consultant or facilitator will soon find the quality of their data degrading if they fail to manage the climate, the sociability and rapport within any group – making critical comments or trying to refocus discussion may be perceived as abrupt or harsh by those in the group. Any perceived insensitivity will ensure that focus group members not only stop providing you with information but will see to it that your style is discussed and shared with their colleagues on their return to their workstation!

Input from focus groups is essential for both the consultant and the client to make an accurate diagnosis. Focus groups can comprise three to eight people. When conducting focus groups make sure that the material you use, in the interview or questionnaire, is designed to check the data and information already to hand, and helps you to identify and isolate the problem you have been engaged to resolve. At this time retrace what has happened before and identify any previous key drivers that caused the present situation.

Your recommendation must directly answer the contract you have with the client. You also need to judge whether other issues arising during the data collection phase ought to be brought to the client's attention. If you are an internal consultant working with an external consultant beware of the external trying to elicit more work before the initial problem has been resolved. Be aware also that the client may not have the resources to address more than one issue at any one time. The degree of rapport you have established, the complexity of the initial brief and the nature of what else you have identified will determine how you address this dilemma.

WHO OWNS THE PROBLEM?

There is an interesting debate about who owns the problem, and the solution. The role of the consultant should be to encourage the client to take the problem sufficiently seriously that they will take ownership. Beware the client who sees the consultant as having a neatly packaged solution. If this is the case the client does not own the problem, or the solution. The consultant must use everything in their power to get the client to accept the reality of the problem as well as committing to the solution. The consultant is available only to help with the diagnosis and to support the client in making decisions.

As a consultant, what body of knowledge are you using to diagnose the problems in the organization? Are you using standard theories that are supported by relevant research? What evidence is there that the actions you prescribe will actually deliver the required results? If you have to tailor a solution, how many options for change are you going to offer the client? If you are an internal consultant charged with delivering a set process or system that is given as a package, what must you do to ensure that the package will fit fully into the organization? If you have free rein over the options, consider whether the organization actually supports the solution. Is the organization ready for the degree of change that you suggest? What is the record of the organization in achieving success with similar programmes?

PHASE 4 – IMPLEMENTATION PLAN
There are several key points to consider here. Is the culture of the organization ready for the solution, and is it capable of sustaining the

evolution of the changes you recommend? When you implement change there will be consequences that spread throughout the business, for example, changes in people's roles, responsibilities and expectations, changes in structure, processes, reporting relationships etc. Have you thought these through? Can the client implement the solution as a 'one-off' event or install the solution as part of a way of life, repeatedly and consistently over years, not just months? Check that the solution fits the client's ability to install. Is the client on the right part of the learning curve? Who will champion, activate and take ownership of the installation and implementation phase? Do the implementers have the necessary skills to deliver the solution, without diluting the message or damaging its credibility? Agree the implementation with the client and the implementer, champion or trainer together with the responsibilities for who does what, when and how.

A plan for implementation should be agreed, and this is best represented as a flow diagram. This plan must incorporate all the behavioural and political activities that are considered prior to the roll-out of the plan. There are a variety of tools that can be used to predict where resistance will lie, and these should be applied to a variety of settings.

Two of the most critical items to be considered at this stage are handling objections to the proposed change and formulating a communications strategy. Objection handling involves identifying those areas where resistance will be highest and ensuring that you fine-tune your plan to anticipate any objections or resistance.

OBJECTION HANDLING

This process works best by identifying the core stakeholders or constituents that can impact on the effectiveness of the intended change. You need to consider the objections that people may have to this process:

- To what extent is the solution politically acceptable to the organization and its key stakeholders? Where is your plan weakest in failing to encounter and overcome the use of 'power politics', when people will wheel and deal resources and horse-trade over control in the business? If people wanted to make mischief and discredit your plan, where would they start and what would they say?

- To what extent is the solution technically feasible? What are the top three technical reasons why this change and implementation plan could be rejected?
- To what extent is the solution economically viable? Will it generate the returns expected? How can you ensure that your contribution is seen as an asset or investment to the organization rather than a liability or drain on resources?
- To what extent are your ideas and the implementation plan relatively simple to install? What action can you take to make the plan easier to install? What support can you offer to help those who doubt your ability to install the ideas and the plan in their particular area of the organization?

COMMUNICATIONS STRATEGY

When driving change, organizations find it impossible 'not to communicate' even if they fail to make any announcements! Even if an organization issues no press releases they are in fact communicating, but at an unconscious level. Not saying anything says a great deal! Choosing not to comment allows people to develop their own response, often fuelled by the grapevine that follows all management action, or inaction. The relative strength of a grapevine can indicate the degree of candour there is in a business. A strong and powerful grapevine indicates the failure of management to create a climate of mutual trust where issues can be debated openly. Creating a formal communications strategy is critical and should be delivered right at the start of the change process. Developing a communications strategy will help you to sell the benefits of the change.

YOU CANNOT NOT COMMUNICATE – DEVELOP A STRATEGY

- List all your key stakeholders.
- For each stakeholder, define what they need to know.
- Design communication precisely to meet the expressed needs of the stakeholder.
- Consider how often you will convey the message.
- How will you test for understanding?
- What medium will convey the communication to best effect?
- Have you assessed the pros and cons of each medium, ie face-to-face communication, briefing meetings, site meetings, open discussion meetings, video presentations etc?
- Who will communicate the message?
- How can you ensure that the message is credible?

Managers often think that it is only appropriate to communicate a message once. They could learn much from their colleagues in Marketing who clearly state that you can only stimulate 'buyer behaviour' when the message has been communicated at least three times. The message has to be conveyed differently, rephrased and, if possible, reinforced by visual imagery. The communication has to generate a positive emotion and be of value to the recipient in terms of making them aware of the information or the message. Most communications strategies operate at the unconscious level; too many assumptions are made and the strategy evolves and is distributed in a random way. Formulating a communications strategy is a detailed process requiring rigorous planning and testing. Management must take charge of the process and control its flow and its intention; it must develop feedback mechanisms to illustrate whether what is communicated is actually supporting and helping the change, or not.

Communicate regularly, frequently and whenever an opportunity offers itself. Always have your 'elevator speech' available (see Chapter 3), the short, sharp communication about the project that can be delivered in 60 seconds.

PHASE 5 – REVIEW, FEEDBACK AND RELENTLESS IMPROVEMENT

The last phase is Review, Feedback and Relentless Improvement. An important part of this phase is measuring progress – the success of the change – and the detail of the implementation plan. Focus on and measure only what can be managed. Measure both 'hard' business and 'soft' cultural issues. When deciding on metrics, focus on changes in the culture and processes as being the main drivers. When developing the measures, discuss them with those who will be affected or involved and, more importantly, those who 'work' rather than those who just manage the process. Build up support. Do not use traditional measures if they send the wrong message. Use new, innovative measures to assess the success of the implementation plan. Help the financial community to understand the new metrics and how they can be tied in to traditional financial measures.

THE CHANGE TEAM – MUTUALLY SUPPORTIVE

There are several characteristics that permeate the client-consultant relationship working through the five phases of the cycle. The consultant, the client and the implementer need to share a high degree of faith, optimism and resilience. They must all believe that the solution will result in improvement, and that it is possible, even if stretch is required for success. The 'critical three' (consultant, client and implementer) should remain positive throughout the ups and downs of the project. The person responsible for this positivity is the internal consultant. As consultant, you must emphasize the benefits of the solution at every opportunity. Be action-orientated and focused on the desired outcomes of implementation. Trust, integrity, credibility and confidentiality are core traits shared by successful internal consultants. Be honest, consistent and approachable to everyone involved in the project. Do not misrepresent the client, or share any misgivings about them with others inside or outside the domain of the client. Actively take steps to demonstrate cohesive and effective teamwork.

Many of the skills of the consultant – behavioural, political and technical – are covered elsewhere in this book. The consultant should actively seek help whenever possible; they cannot be fully competent in every skill. In a unionized environment the consultant should always recognize the value of employees' representatives and work directly with them, the client and the implementers to consolidate a total team approach to the work.

In order to create tools to measure progress you can either tailor your own or buy them 'off the shelf'. My preference is always to tailor them to individual needs because no two organizations are the same. If looking for inspiration for such tools, there are several key sources of information readily available in most organizations. These include surveys of climate, employees, customers and suppliers, and competitive analysis and benchmark studies using clearing-houses and research reports.

Finally, at the start of any project it is useful to prepare a checklist to use against each individual phase of the work. To construct such a list you may wish to review the terms associated with the psychological contract. Client and consultant should approach each meeting in a positive, enthusiastic manner and encourage the same enthusiasm from everyone with whom they come into contact. This will provide your client with a sense of comfort, of trust in your ability to deliver a well thought out, well organized and well planned solution compatible with the client's expectations.

SUMMARY

Action Research helps us to examine how better to plan all the activities that will lead to successful change. In this chapter we have examined the principles behind the Kolb approach to working with specific preferences in mind. We then moved on to a detailed view of the Consulting Cycle and, in particular, how consultant and client can work together more effectively. We have identified the critical issues around which a strong change team should be formed. It is important that the consultant – both external and internal – works well with the client as well as the implementers of change. 'Implementers' are champions of change; we have outlined their role in continually spreading the message.

- Developing a systematic approach is central to implementing change. Doing so – incorporating technical, behavioural and political issues – will make the change successful.

- Confronting potential problems before they arise is the secret to minimizing potential resistance.
- Understand your preferences for problem solving because you may overuse these when many other capabilities are available.
- In many businesses the capability within the organization to drive change is poor because there has been little development of those who manage; their technical specialism is valued but if skills were developed to include 'change management' they could contribute so much more.
- Use the five-phase Consulting Cycle to examine the key issues that need to be resolved around the client, the consultant (external and internal), implementers and stakeholders in the process.
- Commit to developing a psychological contract; this will enable the consultant to achieve more and reduce any potential conflicts with the client. Build rapport with the client early in the process.
- Recognize the value of the internal consultant, even when an external consultant is used.
- Understand the importance of establishing the expectations of everyone who is central to the change team.
- Take the appropriate amount of time during the 'Entry and Contracting' phase to build a good foundation for what is to follow.
- Identify as many symptoms as possible to secure the best solution.
- Use the client's people to help collect data and information.
- Use qualitative as well as quantitative techniques of data collection.
- Triangulate your data and information to ensure accuracy and appropriateness.
- Check for the acceptability of your solution along the political, technical, economic, administrative and cultural dimensions.
- Build a culture of mutual trust and create a true image of integrity as a consultant.
- Never have a crisis of confidentiality.
- Feedback is essential for measuring progress and the level of acceptance of any change. Assess feedback from multiple layers of the business and from many locations and functions.
- Always review and research the material on which you base your diagnosis.

- Theory is vanity, implementation is sanity! Concentrate on making things happen faster.
- Develop a solid communications strategy. Be confident in the knowledge that we are yet to find an organization that over-communicates their key messages to their constituents.
- Develop an organizational commitment to measure what has most impact on performance.
- Commit to a performance-driven culture.
- Focus on Relentless Improvement.
- Communicate at every possible opportunity throughout your client's organization.

6

Cultural Analysis

As an internal consultant you need to work through and understand the complex dynamics of change from an individual, team and organizational perspective. To diagnose problems in a business culture you really need to understand its composition, and how cultures can change. We will focus our thoughts on precisely this subject before turning our attention to examining specific methods and models you can use to develop a clear understanding of how to influence the direction of that culture to support improved business performance. This chapter is an introduction to this important subject.

This analysis helps us to stand back and assess the success and operation of our own organization because it is an attempt to examine the predominant culture within the business. It is a useful exercise to assess the organization's strengths and weaknesses, and to consider what action must be taken to build a strong organization.

UNDERSTANDING CORPORATE CULTURE

The whole concept of organizational culture is often misunderstood. It is vital that we understand the key determinants of corporate culture and any actions that can be taken to shape the culture for enhanced business performance.

In many companies culture evolves slowly and is shaped by key actors, critical incidents and events in the organization's history. Not many people understand the concept of 'culture change'; some even have difficulty understanding the word 'culture' and, more importantly, how it can be managed. This is because a business culture cannot be seen or touched. It is intangible, but it is nonetheless real. We all know what it is like to work within a culture. We know whether a culture is positive or negative, empowering or fear driven; but sometimes we have difficulty defining it. Culture means different things to different people. Explore and examine the key determinants of culture and how it can be changed for the better. Bear in mind that most corporate cultures are not designed or shaped deliberately, most have evolved by accident not design. In order to create a strong culture you need to understand the dynamics of culture change – the culture's key components and how these shape that culture at any point in time.

CULTURE – THE ICEBERG METAPHOR

The reason the iceberg is used as an analogy for corporate culture is fairly self-evident. Like an iceberg, the culture of a business is not openly observable. Just as 90% of an iceberg is submerged beneath the waves so the culture of the organization is not visible to the naked eye. It is our task as external or internal consultants to make the concept of culture visible to our clients so that they can change and shape it for the better. On the surface there are several places in a business where the culture is directly observable. For example, how visitors are greeted when they first approach the reception desk, the response rate and speed at which enquiries are addressed from customer service departments, the office lay-out, the company restaurant, corporate logos, job titles, the allocation of car parking spaces etc all tell us something about the culture of the business. They can indicate whether the place is a pleasant environment in which to work, or not. We constantly pick up on a variety of stimuli about what it might be like to transact business, or work, with an organization. The culture also tells us something about the company. Our thoughts and feelings about a business are shaped by what we see, hear and feel – consciously and unconsciously. The resulting perceptions may indicate and shape our thoughts and opinions about a business on the surface, but they won't enable us to undertake an advanced diagnostic of the company. Nor from our brief exposure to the business can we predict its performance, ability to win new customers or change.

To take the iceberg analogy further, the deeper beneath the waves we go the more difficult it is to identify real, tangible elements of the culture. For the average person there is some difficulty in defining, seeing and touching the culture, although we do still form perceptions about what we experience. We will form an impression of whether it is strong or weak, positive or negative, but this is only a perception to unskilled observers. As a consultant you will have to understand how to shape the culture to support change. It is critical for anyone involved in the change management process to identify the key drivers that shape the business culture.

An organization will continually be displaying symbols or communicating certain 'messages' that reflect its culture. However, the unskilled and inexperienced will need guidance to fully understand the true dynamics to bring about change.

WHAT IS IT ABOUT THE CULTURE THAT CAN SHAPE EVENTS?

It is difficult to establish precisely what it is within any business culture that produces a specific outcome or event. Only by studying the major drivers that shape the culture are we able to understand what action needs to be taken to orchestrate events. An organizational culture can be shaped to become a powerful business by understanding its composition and the dynamics of how it can be changed. Later we will explain the key determinants of corporate culture and the actions to take to build a strong culture.

ONE CULTURE OR MANY?

Any organization can have a central dominant culture, or many diverse cultures. If an organization has many varied and diverse cultures then the ability to manage the ambiguity that can arise is the core challenge of the management team. This can be a major challenge to a consultant who encounters a variety of cultures, all operating under different rules.

Multiple cultures will exist at any one time and be driven by specific circumstances. Many factors shape the formation of a particular cultural hinterland, and our journey is to find out what consultants can do to create a culture that supports any change.

CULTURE – STRONG OR WEAK, POSITIVE OR NEGATIVE?

Business cultures can be categorized along a number of dimensions; they may be perceived as strong or weak, positive or negative, team or process driven. Some cultures are strong and forceful, but this does not necessarily mean that they are also positive and have excellent morale. I have consulted in very powerful, business-driven cultures that achieve results but have the downside of sometimes being negative, punitive and fear driven – not ideally suited for everyone. So, although there can be some aspects of the culture which are favourable it does not mean that all aspects may be viewed in the same positive light. At this point it is important to understand that a thorough cultural review will assess precisely the culture or cultures we are working with. Culture change is a complex issue, and one that can be addressed on a number of different levels, using a variety of tools.

SO WHAT SHAPES CORPORATE CULTURE?

When a business is first created the founders or owners of the business are its chief architects, carefully crafting the mission of the organization to meet its objectives. The views, personal values and passions of the creators are often evident in 'how things are organized'. Over time, the 'how things are organized' can become the norm, the standard of acceptable behaviour for organizing, managing or dealing with issues. As the organization grows, key individuals shape events, deal with crises, set up new processes, restructure the business if necessary and hire new people as required; this all feeds and changes the culture. Senior managers and key players intervene, and their motives and behaviours become evident in the day-to-day operation of the business. If these behaviours are repeated over time they become habits, the norm. In some cases these behaviours are translated into organizational systems and protocols. In other words, the behaviours and actions of influential actors in the company shape how it deals with issues and creates the definition of organizational culture – 'how we do things around here'. What we don't know is, is this for better or worse for the culture?

HOW DO INCONSISTENT CULTURES EVOLVE?

Inconsistent cultures evolve when a number of key players have different rules, or display different values in how they operate and how they manage. This is the norm in cultural development where the culture is shaped by managers' actions agreeing on 'what is important' and 'what is not important'. Failure to understand that there is a strong need for consistency across the organization can lead to major problems. If key players in the business fail to agree on a set process of 'how to do business', then different cultures will emerge within the company, with potentially dire consequences.

For example, the Finance department of a company may display firm regulatory control which produces a strong culture where attention to detail and conformity to protocols and systems are applied rigorously. In the same business, staff in Marketing may value taking major risks in a volatile market. Sales people may be focused entirely on generating revenue by promising more than the production people can deliver. Here we have a business that has an inconsistent culture, a culture that sends out mixed messages both within the business and to its customers. If key players fail to take account of these issues there will be major conflicts within the organization. Each part of the business has different values and can often operate in spite of other parts of that business – playing by different rules – but they won't be able to do so effectively for long. What we can deduce from this example is that there will be a strong misalignment in the organization, resulting in a failure to achieve its overall objectives.

This is what happens in most organizations. A variety of cultures or sub-cultures exist, each driven by the values of key managers. These problems are evident because the key actors and individual managers in the business have structured their part of the business on the basis of their own personal values – those things that are important to them. In the absence of a grander design, managers behave exactly in this way. Any resultant conflict is accidental. No one committed to designing the culture that way, it 'just happened'. In this example, the culture needs rigorous realignment.

CULTURAL ISSUES – APPRAISE YOUR CORPORATE CULTURE

Apply these concepts to your own organization, and think through some of the following issues:

- When communicating with the outside world, on what does your organization focus most attention?
- When communicating with staff and customers, which aspects of the organization appear strong and which appear weak?
- What words best describe how you do business? How would people in different functions define the business?
- How does the organization signal what sort of behaviour is encouraged?
- On the following dimensions, how would you describe your culture?

Positive	Negative
Strong	Weak
Slow	Fast
Vibrant	Tired
Driven for customers	Driven solely by cost
Listening and responsive	Ego-driven and telling
Outgoing and open	Reserved and private

It is interesting to consider how others, occupying key positions in the business, would place your organization. And for the really brave manager, how would staff and external customers appraise the business?

THE CULTURAL ICEBERG

We will examine how cultures can be shaped, but first it is important to develop the core model that will help us understand the dominant drivers behind culture. For the sake of simplicity we can see the Iceberg model as comprising six levels of factors representing cause-effect relationships. Each factor will in turn influence other factors within the culture.

Corporate Culture – The Iceberg Model

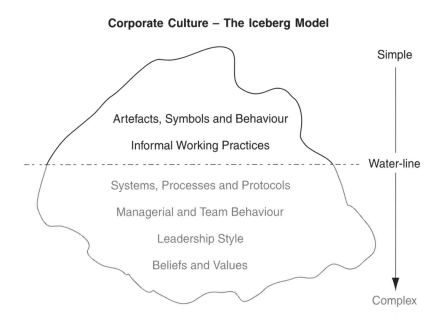

The iceberg model is reflected in the diagram. Fundamentally, the beliefs and values shape the culture of the business. These are usually derived from the philosophy of how and why the organization was originally created. Most organizations are shaped by people who have a clear vision of the future. Even organizations that are created by government through legal mechanisms, working parties and regulatory bodies will nonetheless be shaped by the values and beliefs of the people who have the desire to create them. A new organization will incorporate at least some of the core beliefs and values of its creators, whether they be in a business, political or social context. Beliefs, like values, are never right or wrong, they are just beliefs. Beliefs tell us what is important to an individual; they highlight a higher moral understanding of how to behave and tell us about how a person perceives the world. Beliefs can shape behaviour. 'Values' are how these beliefs are organized and ranked in an individual's consciousness; they are significant factors in shaping behaviour, hence the expression 'People do what they value and value what they do'.

CORPORATE BELIEFS AND VALUES SHAPE BEHAVIOUR

If you spend time talking with a top team of a business try and find out their shared beliefs, then rank order these after testing for understanding; you will now be in a good position to predict the behaviour of this team. In this example, let's look at five beliefs that are owned by two different business teams.

One team has rank ordered their beliefs as:

- Customer focused
- Team driven
- Supportive of personal development
- Focused on commercial success
- Focused on achievement.

Another team has ordered their beliefs as:

- Driven by profit
- Cost reduction as a tool of Continuous Improvement
- Setting goals and objectives
- Strict lines of command
- Loyalty.

These two teams will react very differently to the same situation. What is important to one team appears unimportant to the other. One belief system is not right and the other wrong, they are just different and indicate that behaviour is guided by what business leaders hold dear. All actions and behaviours are guided by beliefs. This is very clear when we see how history in a specific business has unfolded and how dominant characters shape events. For example, most organizations will have experienced traumatic events because of the acts or omissions of a significant character at some stage in their development. These incidents create certain 'beliefs' that people share about whether what happened was good or not. These beliefs continue to have a marked effect on how people 'should' and 'do' work, long after the event is over and the actor or orchestrator has moved on. The beliefs become the culture of the business, the mythology that guides behaviour. People in the organization are driven by their beliefs. Understand beliefs and values before analyzing behaviour.

HOW BELIEFS SHAPE LEADERSHIP STYLE

Whatever beliefs are held by key players in a business will impact upon how they lead, and consequently, on how they manage. The personally held beliefs and values of 'key actors' in an organization are critical in shaping how they lead others. Only when managers understand the importance of values and beliefs will they be able to understand the real complexities of diagnosing and reshaping organizational culture. It is obvious that the leadership will in turn impact upon how the culture evolves; change the leader and the culture will change. A change in personnel can also change the culture. Lose a poor performer and recruit a great team player and the culture will change for the better. Lose a strong leader and inherit a weak manager and the culture will get worse. A key issue here is 'Without leadership there is no change'. Those in the role of consultant need to be aware of the strong relationship between changing a culture and inculcating a strong leadership style.

NOTHING CHANGES UNTIL BEHAVIOUR CHANGES – SHAPING BEHAVIOUR

The consultant and client are key leaders in bringing about change. Others in the business pay attention to what leaders do. As a consultant, understanding and creating a strong leadership style should be at the forefront of your development agenda. A strong style of change leadership can add direction and alignment to an organization, whereas a weak or indifferent style can create confusion and ambiguity. If you have a broadly consistent style of leadership then certain norms will be created within the organization and these norms will become the expected standards of behaviour. This begins to break down when there is a misalignment of styles or where styles exist, evolve and develop by accident. This is very much a 'default' style of management where individual styles, based only upon past experience and without guidance, are applied.

If you want to change the business quickly, work on leadership.

We are all aware of managers who manage by staying within their comfort zone. They are absorbed in the technical nature of their job and don't attempt to influence events. This is the challenge for many companies, to move towards developing a variety of effective leadership styles that enable the organization to change quickly and smoothly.

BEHAVIOUR-SHAPING SYSTEMS

Form follows action. Without action there is no process, no system and no protocols. The behaviours that people display provide guidance on developing standards. These standards can then help to outline formally how we transact business.

As we move upwards towards the tip of the corporate iceberg more and more of the culture becomes visible, and much of it becomes tangible. The next level is focused upon the 'informal way of working', which in turn is very much dictated by the formal system. It is best typified by the climate that keeps people late at the office and gets them into work early. The informal organization is basically the sum total of the informal agreements and the atmosphere which people create amongst themselves to facilitate closure on processes.

The informal system or organization compensates for what the formal system neglects. The informal organization makes things tick and people take personal responsibility to go beyond the bounds of their job description. The health of an organization is often discernible at the level of the informal organization, and can be measured using tools such as attitude surveys, which take into account the motivations, morale and climate of the business. Just being exposed to the informal organization will often tell the careful consultant and researcher more about the culture than owners or senior managers are aware. By talking with people the perceptive student of culture change can develop hypotheses about the nature of organizational problems, and how to improve performance. They will focus upon the cause-effect relationships within the culture that need to be assessed and reshaped. Finally, at the tip of the iceberg we may witness the artifacts and symbols that demonstrate the reason for the organization to exist.

HOW CAN WE ASSESS THE NEED TO CHANGE THE CULTURE?

There are various tools and approaches that can be used; I would like to refer to one particular model, the work of Roger Harrison and Charles Handy, which focuses upon using a four culture classification. When my colleagues and I consult with clients we use a variety of self-designed tools that incorporate cultural surveys, customer reviews, leadership profiles, teamworking questionnaires, focus group workshops etc. Now, more on the Harrison-Handy[10] approach.

This powerful diagnostic tool for measuring culture came from the work of Roger Harrison, with further and later contributions from Handy. Handy has probably done more to propagate this analysis of organizations so we will quote from his approach. Handy suggests that we can classify organizations into four broad cultures. The formation of a particular culture will depend upon a whole host of factors including: company history, ownership, organization structure, technology, critical business incidents, environment, mergers, acquisitions and all the events that have shaped the business you operate in just now.

The four cultures Handy discusses are Power, Role, Achievement (or Task) and Person. The purpose of the analysis is to assess the degree to which the predominant culture reflects the way the organization operates. Some cultures allow for change more readily than others. Some cultures need radical revision to make them truly customer focused. An interesting way to portray the cultures is through symbols, and Handy uses four symbols to differentiate the business cultures.

The Power Culture – The Spider's Web

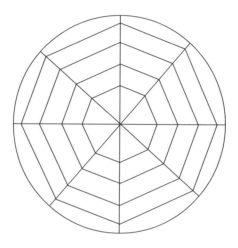

THE POWER CULTURE

The Power culture can be described as a web. This reflects the concentration of power of a family-owned business, of any size. It could be descriptive of the Fiat empire or the small restaurant on the corner. The generic concept of the family business is personified in its extreme by nepotism, with positions of power and core responsibilities being bestowed on family members. There are other powers at play here; some people hold their positions in the company because of *who* they are rather than *what* they know. This creates the strong power structure of the web.

CASE STUDY
POWER RESIDES IN WHO YOU KNOW NOT WHAT YOU KNOW

The power in an organization may reside at the highest level of the business but is not shared equally amongst the people at the top.

Working in Financial Services on a cultural change project, I worked closely with the CEO and the HR Director. It soon became clear that these two individuals controlled the rest of the board – four other members. What was interesting was examining the career paths of high flyers in the business. In nearly every case those who occupied senior or middle management positions were all very close and were associated with the two key men at the top. Although this organization was very team-orientated and worked as an 'Achievement culture' overall, at the top of the board of management the dominant culture was the Power model, based only upon the network of trusted advisors, colleagues and key people in the business.

A key learning point here is that, in this organization, the Power culture worked; however, in many others it does not. It can be solely determined by the intention and morality of those in key positions.

Power of control and authority to influence is concentrated within a small area/group of decision makers, the centre of which is the wheel, or the centre of the web. Power radiates out from the centre (usually displayed by a key personality) to others in the 'family' who send information on through the various networks, functions or units in the business. The term 'family' can be used here literally, for example, the Rothschild's banking empire, and also metaphorically where strong, like-minded personalities gel and become the influencers within the business. Because power and decision making is concentrated in so few hands, the strategists and key family members create situations that others have to deal with and implement. It is difficult for anyone outside of the family network to influence events.

The ability of the Power culture to adapt to changes in the environment is very much determined by the perception and ability of those who occupy the positions of power within it. The Power culture places more faith in individuals than committees, and can either rapidly see the need for change and adapt, or totally fail to see the need for change and collapse.

Where in the organization does the Power culture reside, if at all? Will it help or hinder you in your efforts to change the business? It can be used to shape the culture quickly and effortlessly if you can connect with the right people whilst maintaining and displaying a high degree of integrity.

The Role Culture – The Greek Temple

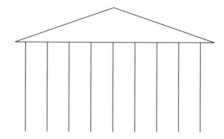

THE ROLE CULTURE

The characteristics and symbolism displayed in the Role culture is very much based upon the large, slow-moving organizations so often associated with government institutions. Bureaucratic is perhaps the best way to describe this culture. The Role culture has been typified as a Greek temple and has often been described as portraying bureaucracy in its purest form. The apex of the temple is where the decision making takes place; the pillars of the temple reflect the functional units of the organization, which have to implement the decisions from the apex. The strength of the culture lies in specialization within its pillars. Interaction takes place between the functional specialisms by means of job descriptions, procedures, rules and systems. This is an organizational culture run on paper systems. Authority is not based upon personal initiatives but is dictated by seniority, job grading, job descriptions and span of control.

Co-ordination is undertaken by a narrow band of senior staff at the top of the organization. This is the only co-ordination required as the system itself provides the necessary integration. Here the job description is more important than the skills and abilities of those who people the culture. Performance beyond the role is not required, or encouraged. The authority of position power is legitimate, personal power is not. This reflects Weber's pure theory of bureaucracy. Systems effectiveness depends upon adherence to principles rather than personalities.

This culture is probably appropriate only in organizations not subject to constant change. Such cultures function well in a 'steady state' environment but are insecure in times of change. Rationality and size typify the Role culture.

As a consultant working in an organization that is largely based upon the Role culture, you will find that progress on change can be slow; you will need to demonstrate considerable patience. Consensus and excessive group processes will govern decision making. The only way to work through a client in this organization is to adhere to the rules and ensure that you understand the process for implementing change, because it is probably documented somewhere in great detail! If a process or methodology does not exist, you will have to make sure that the process that underpins your work is detailed and has been presented to all parties required to approve the process.

However, you may encounter this culture in a larger business that does not as a whole typify the Role culture. This could be a single department that processes routine business but has to ensure that quality is 100% assured. This may reflect some production processes, Finance, some areas of Systems or IT support.

THE ACHIEVEMENT OR TASK CULTURE

The Achievement (or Task) culture is characteristic of organizations that are involved in extensive research and development activities, or in businesses that require complex interactions in order to deliver to demanding customers. Any business that needs a high degree of interaction based upon expert input, orchestrated with precision, would typify this culture. Working as a consultant in such a business can be stretching and mind expanding.

The Achievement or Task Culture – Network Matrix

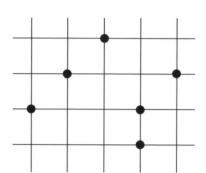

The culture is dynamic; it is constantly subject to change and has to create temporary task or project teams to meet anticipated (or unanticipated) demands on the business. Information and expertise are valued here. This culture is represented visually by a net or latticework. Close liaison between departments, functions and specialisms is critical. Liaison, communication and integration are the means whereby the organization can anticipate and adapt to change quickly.

Where the team culture is focused primarily on results, influence is based upon expertise and up-to-date information. This culture employs real experts, and positions of power reside in areas where strands of knowledge are instantly brought together.

This is a truly dynamic environment for the consultant. Probably the biggest challenge in many businesses today is introducing this fast-moving culture.

THE PERSON CULTURE

The Person culture is characteristic of the consensus model of management, where the individuals within the structure collectively determine the path to take. If there is a formalized structure it tends to service the needs of the individuals within the structure. Organizations displaying this culture reject formal hierarchies and exist solely to meet the needs of their members. The rejection of formal management control and reporting relationships suggests

The Person Culture – Loose Connections

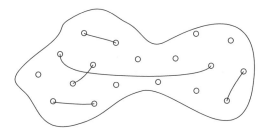

that this may be a suitable culture for a self-help group, commune or co-operative, not for a large business. This culture tends to exist in the 'not-for-profit' sector and can include healthcare and voluntary organizations, sports and social groupings. This type of culture is also well represented in small business communities such as Training, Consultancy and Marketing where personal development and commitment to a cause are more important than a strict focus on business improvement.

Consulting in this type of business can be very rewarding. In general, people who are attracted to this type of culture are committed to personal development, learning and any contribution they can make to the organization's success. As a consultant, if you can win the client over to developing more structure in the way they manage change this would improve performance. Often, winning commitment is not the problem, the problem is being able to apply business principles to the passion.

APPROPRIATE CULTURES

Handy's typologies of organizational structure suggest that we should try, whenever possible, to match the culture with the external demands and constraints on the organization. Bear in mind that different operating units within the organization require different structures. Some units or functions will be operating in a 'steady state' environment where there are few changes and the future is reasonably predictable; others will be subject to a great deal of change, not only in what they do but also in how they do it. It is therefore important to have different approaches to managing different 'cultures' in different units. The four characteristics, which determine the culture of departments and functions, are stated below:

A **Crisis/Breakdown** environment refers to decisions which have to be made quickly and which impact upon the long-term effectiveness of the organization. This environment requires a 'power-orientated' culture.

A **Research & Development** environment demands constant change. The process of creating innovation is also important. Experts have to be taken from key areas and moulded together to reach a project objective. The Achievement culture is geared to this activity.

The **Steady State** environment typifies the repetitive duties in which all organizations have to engage in order to remain efficient. These may include accounting procedures, selection, recruitment, salary and wage administration, inventory control, maintenance etc. A culture based upon the predictability and procedural approach of the Role culture would appear to meet the needs of the function.

The **Policy Making** environment refers to the creation of long-term plans for the company. If policy making is perceived as an interactive process, the Task culture seems the most fitting. Secrecy and security may make this culture prone to the Power orientation.

Charles Handy suggests that different units, which pursue different activities, should adopt a culture that reflects their needs. For example, bookkeepers working in a steady state climate, where their work is predictable, will probably function best in a Role culture. A research unit will need to project an Achievement culture, but would not work effectively with a Power, Role or Person culture.

Managing cultures is difficult in large organizations, especially if you have to interact with other units with different cultures. As a consultant, imagine the problems involved in trying to influence a Customer Services manager from a Role culture to work on a task team with the Chief Accountant from a Power culture, to discuss the implementation of an Achievement culture! You need to think about what sort of culture you need to operate in normally, as well as the predominant culture you will be working within for particular projects.

CONSULTING ACROSS CULTURES

Consultants must understand the concept of culture and how it impacts upon their performance in driving change and working with others on the change team. As a consultant it is vital that you learn to cope with people from different business cultures.

A process improvement initiative may work in a steady state environment such as 'Financial Management', but the same initiative could fail in a Marketing or Sales unit where circumstances cause cultures to change rapidly. It is not the initiative that is important, but how it is structured to fit the environment. Those driving change need to concentrate resources on managing across departmental boundaries rather than top-down through functions. Pursue this approach and change can be implemented very quickly.

CULTURAL CHANGE AND MANAGING THE TRANSITION

Simply knowing what culture is desirable and engendering the key values, reflected by consistent managerial behaviour, will not of itself create the change you desire. You still have to manage the transition from one state to the other. Change takes time, and can stimulate considerable resistance. Understanding the changes which staff go through, their likely behaviour, their perception of the situation and the support they require is demanding.

Elisabeth Kubler-Ross[11] has researched how people come to terms with change. Her research involved investigating the stages and behaviours displayed by people coping with terminal illness: Shock – Denial – Unlearning – Relearning – Integration. Similarly, other researchers have spent time exploring how people come to terms with radical changes in their life including divorce, alcoholism, bereavement, redundancy etc. We have a great deal to learn from this research. Much of it is applicable to organizational situations, but we do not have space here to explain the subject to the depth required. It is, however, necessary for the change agent to invest time in examining the major stages people go through when involved in significant organizational change, and a good starting point is the work of Kubler-Ross.

SUMMARY

This introduction to corporate culture has suggested that a culture is difficult to define because it lacks substance and tangibility. The iceberg analogy is useful because it suggests that the deeper the thinking we employ, the more we can identify the drivers which shape culture. Culture is discussed frequently in change management circles, but few really understand the dynamics of creating a strong culture. A business culture is shaped by the values that drive the business, and these reflect the personal values and beliefs of the business's creators or founders. Strong and purposeful values can create a dominant leadership style that is replicated many times over, becoming common practice for all levels of managers and team leaders. Leadership behaviour translates into what is acceptable and what is not, the informal 'standards of performance' that drive the business are quickly created. Observable, but undocumented, these standards will reflect the culture of the business and will shape a culture geared more for performance improvement. It is imperative that the change agent becomes a 'master' of corporate culture and always examines change in terms not just of the individual personalities involved, or even the teams, but also of the larger issue of the culture.

- An organization cannot not have a culture. However, the top team can choose how to shape it.
- The beliefs of the owners or founders of the organization will initially shape its direction, mission and culture.
- As an organization evolves the culture will change; either it can be directed deliberately or it will evolve through chance and circumstance.
- Culture change should be a deliberate process.
- Leadership style is critical in shaping behaviour.

- Nothing changes until behaviour changes. Managers should be role models.
- Over-reliance on systems, Process Mapping and protocols will never compensate for an enduring focus on deliberate and planned culture change.
- The most visible part of the business culture probably reflects what needs to be examined at a much deeper level. Analysis at this level should generate the right questions to be asked.
- Weak cultures can become easily manipulated by key people.
- Cultures are shaped by people – by their values, thoughts, beliefs and actions.
- Examine the dominant factors that shape your own business, and compare your views with those of others in the business.
- If you can start to understand the determinants of culture then you can define it. If you can define it, you can measure change. If you can measure changes in the culture, then you can shape it!

Assessing the Style of the Client

This chapter focuses on the importance of developing interpersonal skills to establish rapport and a close working relationship with all those involved in the process of change. In particular, it focuses on the client as the target for persuasion; however, the information presented could equally be applied to anyone whom the consultant is keen to influence. First we will look at enabling a variety of people to change, but focus primarily on the implementers – the people we are trying to influence to implement the key ideas within the organization. Then we will focus on influencing the client and discovering which domain they inhabit – Regulator, Visionary, Facilitator or Analyst.

DEVELOPING MUTUAL TRUST – CHANGE BASED ON PERSUASION AND INFLUENCE NOT CONTROL

Many internal consultants rely far too much on control rather than persuasion and influence, especially when it comes to handling implementers; this is a mistake. Consultants may think that the position they hold with a client is sufficient to ensure that people will comply with their wishes. This may be true in a fear-driven culture, but in the vast majority of cases the consultant has to win support at every level. Managing a project successfully requires more than brute force. Today, control is no longer recognized as a legitimate means of initiating organizational change. Change is more a process of involvement and trust; the skills of persuasion and influence are key. We can distinguish the traditional process of managing change as being imposed or driven by 'telling', and generally associate this approach with a failure to bring about long-term change.

THE OLD WAY OF CHANGE

The days are gone when 'change' was ordered by senior management, where control and unquestioned adherence to authority, personified in the managerial group, was sacrosanct. This way of doing business was unquestioned by the recipients or the implementers of change. This classical or scientific management view of business believed that control was the sole province of the managerial group. Such a view may still survive today, but it lacks credence. In this type of organization there is a gulf – in terms of power, control and influence – between those who manage resources and those who do the majority of the work. In this outmoded managerial model the managerial prerogative is to dictate and direct people to meet the specific needs of the organization. Things are changing, but slowly. A better approach is to be more open to examining other forms of relationships between those who manage and those who do the work.

Thankfully, trends in social convention and attitudes have been responsible for changing views on how to motivate people. The more directive, 'telling' style has been replaced with a 'selling' style. The old style is characteristic of a fear-driven culture, where the only way to manage people was 'carrot and stick' – through reward and sanction rather than influence. Employees increasingly refuse to be managed in this way and consciously look to work in more progressive organizations.

EFFECTIVE CHANGE

Change tends to be more effective and long lasting if those involved and affected have a significant part to play in the process. The consultant has an important role here, influencing others to want to become involved in the process, rather than just telling them what to do. Increasingly, this is becoming the most important area of the process of change management – establishing rapport and a true spirit of teamwork with those driving change.

In order to be effective, the consultant (internal or external) needs to be able to work closely with everyone in the team. The consultant has to be able not only to develop rapport but also to retain it, even in times of conflict. Developing rapport involves understanding how people communicate, and their preferences for assessing, accepting and agreeing with you – the consultant. This means exploring and understanding how people process information and their likely preferences for action, so that you can influence them.

A PREREQUISITE FOR DRIVING CHANGE – INTERPERSONAL SKILLS

In our consultancy work my colleagues and I use an interpersonal skills model to help internal consultants understand the dynamics that exist between the key actors in the consultation process. We take staff through an intensive training programme lasting several days. An outline of this process follows. (Please note, we work on training others in advanced forms of interpersonal influence including Neuro Linguistic Programming.) One of the most powerful tools we offer is a dynamic model of Personality and Communication. The model focuses on the differences that exist between different personality types. If there is a wide variation in how people communicate with one another then there is a greater risk of conflict. Generally, people like people like themselves. However, in the work environment we are forced to encounter a wide diversity of characters. We aim to understand how different personalities communicate and to recognize any areas for potential conflict. The model[12] is simple to understand. It is based upon just two personality characteristics – those related to how people use power and how they use emotion when communicating with others.

As stated previously, fundamental to this approach is the belief that 'people like people like themselves', and like-minded individuals will tend to find and share a deeper level of rapport with one another. People who experience wide differences between their style and that of colleagues will find it much harder to work together because they value different communication approaches. The view that 'opposites attract' is best left to the world of romance! As a general rule, we are attracted to people who display similar characteristics to ourselves. People tend to be attracted to, and work more effectively with, people who share and value similar mindsets and ways of working.

A great deal of the training we offer consultants progresses through the following process:

1 Identify your own style; explore and understand your strengths and weaknesses when communicating with a variety of people. This requires the critical ability to assess when 'displaying own style' will lead to conflict with people portraying the 'opposite' style. The best way to assess this is to complete the questionnaire in this chapter (see p139) and then ask others to view and comment on your results. However, looking back at your behaviour or the behaviour of others in difficult situations usually points the way to identifying your dominant style.

2 Identify the style of the people you wish to influence, and anticipate their possible objections to your proposal. This demands a high degree of conscious competence in picking up the preferences of others, using our recommended model. With coaching and training this competence – scanning for and listening to the phrases, words, tonality and body language of others – can be acquired. Most importantly, there is a need for high 'sensory acuity', focused on looking for congruent communication.

3 Re-appraise the purpose and context of the communication from the point of view of the person you are trying to influence. Rethink; adjust your message to suit their preferences, their world.

4 Deliver the message in the manner and context in which 'others' prefer to receive it; listen to their responses.

The model is based on four 'pure' types – the Regulator, the Visionary, the Facilitator and the Analyst. Of course, there are many more than four types of personality in existence, but this model can be extremely useful for dealing with objections before communicating formally with those we seek to influence. In this sense I use it as a tool for preventing misunderstanding and gaining rapport with clients, implementers and other stakeholders.

I believe that people intuitively have their own classification system by which they assess others; this is usually an unspecific, unconscious process and therefore difficult to apply consistently. I find that the following methodology helps to improve assessment of the key characters, and their personalities, in the change arena. It therefore helps us in preparing to influence these key characters before the event takes place. In my view, too few people spend time examining their ability to influence, beyond the simple and rational basis of their argument. Remember to bear in mind context, and remain flexible. No one person portrays one style all the time. Although they may have one strong preference when communicating, the context of the communication will shape how they move from one style to another.

The communication style displayed is based upon personal preferences as well as context and circumstances, the demands and constraints of the situation. No one stays in a single style all the time, they move about. The key to becoming a change master is having the sensory acuity to follow as the person you are trying to influence moves from one style to another. In any interaction the person with the most flexible communication will have more strategies and greater ability to influence others and will therefore tend to be at an advantage most of the time.

IDENTIFYING INFLUENCING STYLE

Use the simple exercise overleaf to gain a good understanding of the four 'pure types' described. This is a simple questionnaire to isolate 'type'. It is for illustration only. More sophisticated and accurate 'profiles' are used to help consultants identify the style of influence with which others feel most comfortable.

Instructions

Tick the word in each pair which best represents how you influence others. Total the ticks in just the left hand column of each word pairing and place on the chart below.

Use of Power (V score)   **Use of Emotion** (H score)

__ Active   __ Steady   __ Laid back   __ Formal

__ Confronts   __ Accepts   __ Lively   __ Unmoved

__ Decisive   __ Studied   __ Random   __ Structured

__ Compete   __ Co-operate   __ Affiliative __ Private

__ Impatient   __ Relaxed   __ Trusting   __ Cautious

__ Challenge   __ Receptive   __ Sociable   __ Distant

__ Direct   __ Indirect   __ Informal   __ Formal

__ Forceful   __ Thoughtful   __ Intuitive   __ Rational

__ Forthright   __ Reflective   __ Friendly   __ Reserved

__ Proactive   __ Reactive   __ Casual   __ Organized

Use of Power (V Score)

	Regulator	Visionary
	Analyst	Facilitator

Use of Emotion (H score)

PEN PORTRAITS OF THE FOUR 'TYPES'

The four quadrants are best explained as follows:

The 'pure' **Analyst** occupies the bottom left quadrant and generally demonstrates little emotion. Tending to introversion, the Analyst will not be drawn into major discussion. Being analytical types, they tend to demonstrate a longer attention span, thinking things through in terms of chains or sequences of events. The Analyst will be focused upon detail, objectivity and technical competence. This type will have difficulty working closely with people who are unlike themselves, especially the Visionary. Analytical types will tend to be influenced more readily by people like themselves and their more assertive colleagues, the Regulators.

The 'pure' **Facilitator** occupies the bottom right quadrant; the type is very receptive as well as extrovert. They will be receptive to the views of others. Unlike the Analysts they will be good team workers. They will want to be liked and may have problems dealing with conflict. Facilitators have some difficulty with Regulators, perceiving them to be emotionless, and can align quite well with their more assertive colleague, the Visionary.

The **Visionary** is very assertive and quite extrovert. Driven by a need to work on new creative projects, Visionaries will move quickly from one idea to another. They will want to be recognized for their achievements and will ensure that others are aware of their successes. They are driven by achievement and developing new solutions to problems. They have difficulty working with Analysts but will have some understanding with their more receptive colleagues, the Facilitators.

The **Regulator**, characterized in the top left quadrant, is very assertive and lacks the outward signs of emotion. Driven by results, Regulators want to be in charge of things. Although they can work on the detail, they prefer to move swiftly from A to Z rather than plodding through A, B, C, D... Z etc. Regulators will have much in common with their less assertive colleague, the Analyst.

These pen portraits give a basic understanding of how the change agent can use the model. Being aware of communication preferences in advance will allow you to structure events to appeal to a variety of audiences.

In order to do a really good job all the change agent really has to do is learn how to use the model, understand the preferences of each type, move around and deal with objections as required. Below is a little more detail on each of the four 'pure' types.

WHAT IS A REGULATOR?

The pure Regulator is assertive and reserved in outlook. Their communication is logical and well structured. Their style lacks emotive overtones. The content of any discussion is usually focused on the matter under consideration; tangential conversation is not displayed or encouraged.

Those on the extreme of the scale can be perceived as lacking warmth, and may be defined as authoritarian. However, this is probably more a reflection of their desire to present and debate topics in an analytical and objective manner. Regulators do not like emotion to cloud the facts or their judgement. They also like to be – and be seen to be – in control of the situation.

The name Regulator encapsulates the style of the communicator; they regulate and control the flow of resources. In their purest form, Regulators can be powerful authoritative figures who do not seek the views of others. Like the Visionary, they have their own views, are fairly confident in their abilities and rely on their own judgement. On the surface, they do not seek the friendship and approval of others. However, they may seek formalized approval of their results from colleagues senior to them.

The Regulator could be classed as emphasizing achievement, wishing to be recognized for results rather than for people skills or idea generation. Although governed and measured by results, the Regulator is not drawn into the minutiae of problems. Like the Visionary, the Regulator prefers to have a global perspective and tends to delegate detailed work to others.

CASE STUDY

WORKING WITH THE 'REGULATOR' AS THE CLIENT

This company manufactured microwave antenna; it was US-owned but located in the UK. The Operations Director was on assignment from the States. I used to meet him once a week to discuss progress on a quality improvement drive. I would arrive at 11am and he would say 'Phil, how are you, and how is the family?' I would reply 'Fine Roy, everything is good. How is your family adapting to the British way of life?' He would then say, 'Fine, that's good news. Now let us move on to the progress report. Tell me, what projects are working? What are the results for each of the project groups? Are there any areas that need my input? Is anyone dragging their feet? What else can we expect for month end; any cost reductions coming through?' I would reply specifically, wasting no time at all. I would be totally accurate and stay 100% on the subject. He would then draw the discussion to a close. 'Phil, it is good to see you. Any concerns you have about progress come and see me. If there is nothing else – have a good week. Bye'. It would be 11.15am when I left his office, never a moment later.

This client was very much a strong Regulator. He wanted focused discussion. He gave the impression of being interested in my family, but he wasn't. The worst thing I could have done was to wax lyrical about each of my children and create unnecessary discussion for him. Adapt to the world of your client! If they move and adopt another style, follow them – but do not lead. Let them determine the flow of discussion and the length of the meeting. For consultants who have clients that display strong or even occasional Regulator tendencies, follow this advice to the letter or you will create doubts in the client's mind about your focus on the business at hand!

As a reserved person, the Regulator will not be a natural team leader. They will tend to issue instructions rather than sell ideas.

As someone expecting action, the last thing on the Regulator's mind is how their ideas may affect their staff. This will only be taken into account when people problems could affect productivity and bottom line results. Regulators are impatient and want to take action *now*; they don't have time to waste. Once you have won their commitment you may have to work quickly; speed is perceived as a positive trait. Slow-paced thinking, being overly thoughtful and an inability to take quick, decisive action will be perceived as weaknesses.

What Objections will the Regulator have to your Proposals?

When presenting to a Regulator you must prepare your case, proposals or recommendations well in advance. Regulators demand relevant and accurate answers. If they ask a question then they expect a speedy reply. Your credibility will be evaluated by your ability to think on your feet.

Regulators expect you to get to the point and not introduce subjects of little relevance. They prefer to be directed from start to finish, no tangents or diversions. Make sure that your proposals are watertight – if they cost too much in terms of money, time or resources the Regulator may not be interested. The 'pure type' Regulator is not just interested in results tomorrow. Although they are interested in long-term objectives, they are aware that they will be measured by short-term criteria.

If you have changes to implement, make sure that your proposals and recommendations can be closely monitored, evaluated and measured after installation. Your proposals shouldn't concentrate on the *features* of any likely changes but rather on their benefits and advantages. All managers can be resistant to change, but Regulators in particular will be resistant to new proposals if it cannot be shown that an initial investment in time and money will lead to worthwhile results.

WHAT IS AN ANALYST?

The 'pure' Analyst is reserved and projects little emotion when communicating. Analysts are introverted and tend to build their reputation around technical expertise rather than managerial ability. They are competent, analytical and methodical by nature. Their approach to examining and solving problems is rational, structured and logical. 'Pure' Analysts are immersed in their technical expertise, whether they are a lawyer, accountant or technical specialist. Analysts are formal in their dealings with others and, unlike their opposites the Visionary and Facilitator, they are not outgoing. They are rather private and cautious, directing and focused upon implementation and technical purity. Their rational manner suggests that they look at problems from a micro-perspective. They don't normally concern themselves with the whole picture but concentrate on the detail. Consequently, when trying to sell an idea or proposal to these people, you first have to focus on the technical feasibility of the suggestion and then the practical aspects.

As well as being reserved in their dealings with other people, Analysts are receptive to what others are saying. They will listen for the technical sophistry. They won't dominate the conversation but will listen carefully, assessing in detail the validity of what is being said. They are thoughtful and reflective and won't make too many assumptions; they will listen and then ask questions to test their understanding. Analysts are steadfast and steady, they prefer not to confront people.

CASE STUDY

WORKING WITH THE 'ANALYST' AS CLIENT

Another client, Richard, was an HR professional who took a keen interest in our approach to culture change. I would visit Richard and always knew things would take longer than planned. He wanted precise detail. He would request that we looked at activities in a Gantt chart format with time-frames clearly legible, expected results and potential measures. Later he would translate this information onto a 'critical path' on his PC, directly routing this to a spreadsheet where he accounted for all budgets that arose from the work undertaken. He would regularly ask for input on improvements and want to express these using time series indexing. He never talked about how the change teams were progressing, except in terms of the processes they applied. For Richard, team harmony and morale were secondary to getting the detail precisely right. Once he asked for a description of my 'culture change process' from A–Z. We took some time to go through the detail and he would interject, 'Take me back to the… I'd like to think through the implications if we changed our focus from a project on materials planning to one on quality assurance'. Often the meetings overran well beyond the projected departure time because Richard needed a great deal of attention and concrete data. Although there were times when I became frustrated with Richard I continued to give him what he wanted, or made sure that I had anticipated his needs and provided an appendix in Gantt chart format!

The learning points with Analysts are that as consultant your credibility is on the line if you cannot demonstrate a logical approach and go to the same depth of analysis as they do.

Analysts are not spontaneous but studied in their approach. Although on the lower extreme of the 'assertiveness' scale, they can be sociable and work with others. When working with a team they have difficulty adjusting to the needs of others, but they are generally co-operative. They are steady and stable. You have to spend considerable time on the technical feasibility of any proposal to convince them; they want to assess its capability and see it work. Analysts have difficulty coping with situations where there is a great deal of information which appears to have little structure; when presenting proposals to an Analyst make sure you prepare carefully and structure your ideas in a logical fashion. Analysts are technically proficient and feel secure when they are confident that they have all the available knowledge on a subject. Their need for this security can be a weakness because many Analysts persist in collecting masses of information to solve problems, rather than being selective. Here you can help Analysts see their way through a mass of detail.

Analysts don't like making decisions based on what they consider to be incomplete information. An inability to make decisions can often result from an aversion to risk taking. They prefer situations where risk is calculable and measurable; they won't get involved in speculative ventures.

Unlike the Visionary, the Analyst has difficulty working with ideas and making them a reality. The 'pure' Analyst prefers to work with quantifiable alternatives. The Analyst sets goals that are achievable, and may have a tendency to focus on short-term objectives. Analysts can concentrate too much on detail and pay scant attention to the long-term or global perspective. When they do become involved in projects that have long-term implications they gain their security by meticulously planning and preparing in advance. They can have difficulty relating to the Visionary because their traits are at the opposite end of the spectrum. The Analyst shares the reflective nature of the Facilitator but does not share their willingness to be expressive, open and trusting in communication.

The Analyst shares the Regulator's reserved stance in communication but is distinguished by a more positive and challenging assertive posture. Analysts have difficulty understanding proposals in broad terms. They need to see the proposal 'as it will operate' and then assess its practicality.

WHAT IS A FACILITATOR?

'Pure' Facilitators are receptive in communication. They listen to what others say, involve people in decisions and discuss proposals at length. They are keen to understand the implications of new or innovative suggestions. They aren't quick to make up their mind and are ready to accept ideas, but generally pursue the indirect route. They want to look at problems from every angle.

The Facilitator will listen carefully to suggestions. The 'pure' Facilitator facilitates the introduction of change and new ideas, but only after thinking through the key issues.

By nature, the Facilitator is a team player and a 'people person'. They want to know how a proposal will affect their staff. Will they require retraining? What impact will changes have on job satisfaction, motivation, team spirit and morale? Facilitators tend towards extroversion and are generally outgoing in manner. Others seek their help as they are generally approachable. Their way of looking at things is different to the Analyst who requires facts, figures and a structured approach to problem-solving. The Facilitator tends to be unstructured; the logic of the Analyst is replaced by intuitive and creative skills.

Creativity and intuition bind Facilitators and Visionaries together, and they find it relatively easy to work with one another. Unlike the Visionary, the Facilitator does not feel a need to dominate conversations. Facilitators don't share the fast-paced and highly demanding objective setting and commitment to achievement of the Visionary or the Regulator.

Regulators and Facilitators can find it hard to communicate effectively with one another. The 'pure' Facilitator can view the 'pure' Regulator as cold, unapproachable, impatient and interested only in results. Conversely, the Regulator can view the Facilitator as unstructured, casual and uncommitted to achieving results. Often these perceptions lead to conflict rather than co-operation.

The Facilitator can become too committed to people and fail to recognize the importance of results. Facilitators have to be convinced that new proposals won't harm people or lead to problems of morale in their team. They are usually strongly affiliative; their popularity with others is the source of their strength and power. Getting Facilitators to take ownership of proposals is tantamount to having them implemented. However, the 'pure' Facilitator will put you through immense rigours to ensure that all people problems are resolved before implementation. Sometimes they lack focus and require others to help structure their thoughts and actions. Although it is possible to lead and structure a 'pure' Facilitator, progress will be slow.

CASE STUDY

WORKING WITH THE 'FACILITATOR' AS CLIENT

Driving a project on leadership in motor finance I worked with an HRD manager who was extremely sociable. James wanted to know all about what motivated me to run a consultancy business. He explored my values and why I liked working with people; he was particularly keen to explore my way of working. On the potential leadership project he wanted to ensure that when I undertook the diagnostic work I would select people for focus groups on a 'fair and equitable basis'. (I was interested in the challenge of undertaking a 'training needs audit' with a selection of staff – new to the business – who had previously experienced problems with a particularly harsh manager.) James was totally focused on us working together symbiotically and had to be reassured that we would discuss all training matters before the training programme was designed. He was extremely supportive but, unfortunately, had prior to my arrival worked with another consultant who had shown impatience with his intense questioning and probing. James wanted to make sure that I was someone with integrity who would consider the people issues at every stage of the assignment, as would he.

The learning points here are that Facilitators may consume huge amounts of time rethinking the people or team issues that relate to a project. Focusing on their concerns, although time-consuming, ensures a long-term commitment to your work as a consultant because you maintain the same high degree of integrity as displayed by the client.

Facilitators with a strong affiliation drive will find it easier to accept proposals from someone they feel close to. Being intuitive they tend to trust their instincts. They don't possess the same abilities as the Analyst. They tend to rely on openness and trust; this can be a weakness if they let friendships, rather than facts, sway their judgement.

WHAT IS A VISIONARY?

A person projecting a Visionary style of communication is both assertive and responsive to new ideas. Visionaries like to tackle new problems and seek innovative solutions. They are enthusiastic and promote changes that reflect their concept of how things should be. When discussing proposals with Visionaries, ask them to explain their ideas, their concepts and rationale. Do not formally oppose or challenge their vision.

Visionaries seek praise and recognition for their ideas, though they often need help to make them a reality. A Visionary is often an extrovert and seeks attention and approval from others. Effective Visionaries are leaders in their field where they have the 'balance' to put their ideas into practice. Because they are assertive, responsive and extrovert in nature, Visionaries can become confused with too many ideas, and have difficulty turning them into reality.

A Visionary does not enjoy dotting the i's and crossing the t's. They would rather concentrate on the bigger picture than get involved with the detail.

CASE STUDY

WORKING WITH THE VISIONARY AS CLIENT

When acting as a consultant with a large software developer I worked closely with a client, Vivian, who was an imaginative Visionary, wanting only to commit to the most innovative thinking. Vivian was originally a software developer who had achieved her PhD in Psychology, had worked her way into the business and had emerged as Change Management Director. She keenly wanted to implement the very best in quality improvement in the business. She was only interested in what was 'unique', 'new' and 'innovative'. The Deming, Crosby, EFQM and other approaches to quality improvement were not attractive. Vivian wanted the most challenging, most esoteric approaches that would demonstrate her drive, flourish and intellect. We worked well together. Meetings were brief and exciting. As consultant, I had to record all our decisions and feed back immediately on what we had agreed. Her quick tangential thinking, low attention span and search for the new and exciting could distract us from our agenda. It was great fun working with her but it meant I had to ensure that closure was agreed on set decisions, while at the same time being open to changing what had gone before.

Key learning from this client was the ability to follow the degree of spontaneity that was displayed and then quickly identify potential shortfalls or problems that could arise from almost instantaneous decision making (which did not involve consulting others in the supply chain).

Because Visionaries can be highly conceptual their ideas can become confused. To communicate effectively with a Visionary you need to listen to what is being said, what is not being said and what cannot be said without help. This should then be reflected back for consideration. A Visionary can come up with loads of good ideas but, without assistance, these ideas may never be transferred to the work situation. We are all tuned into ideas, proposals and recommendations that reflect our outlook on life. To avoid alienating the Visionary we may have to rethink our ideas and present them in a different way, one that is novel and innovative.

SOME THOUGHTS ON USING THE FOUR 'TYPE' APPROACH

Every client can prove to be a challenge. The model outlined here helps us understand how the client views the world. Remember, the client will move around the matrix of the four pure types each and every day as contexts and situations change. As consultant, you have to be aware of the client moving from one type to another. The key learning point is being able to identify when clients are displaying these different behaviours and then adapt your behaviour quickly. You should also use this approach with others in the change team. As consultant, there will be times when you will be running a presentation or workshop and come across these four types, all in the same event! You will quickly have to develop the flexibility to respond to them, not as you see the world and the impact and effect of these changes, but to appeal to their preferences.

SUMMARY

In summary, the model presented is only a model to help understand social interaction. I find it helps people to structure their formal and informal presentations and discussions. It forces the influencer, the 'consultant', to think through discussions before entering into them. This enables the consultant to anticipate core objections to proposals and helps build a stronger case from the perspective of all 'types of people'.

Finally, a word to those of you who think such an approach smacks of manipulation. Of course, this model gives the sender of the communication or influencer more leverage with those whom they would seek to influence.

It would be relatively easy to use the model to manipulate people into situations, but our purpose in understanding the model is to influence with integrity. As long as our purpose is accepted by others as being just and well intentioned, then we can feel free to use the approach to help us push change in a direction which will benefit all. Remember, understanding how others view our proposals forces us to develop more flexible, win-win solutions.

- As a consultant, first understand your own style before attempting to influence others.
- Before you try to influence people in the change team think through the 'triggers' which turn each of the four pure types on or off a project. Work out in advance how you can handle objections from each of the four types.
- When presenting a proposal to a selection of the four pure types or styles, sell the benefits from the perspective of each type.
- Present a coherent view of the changes and the benefits that will accrue for each member of the change team. For example, lead with the effect on bottom line results then follow up with an offer to talk through the detail if required. You may then wish to discuss how this approach compares to other new and existing solutions or ideas and finish off with the people perspective. Here you have dealt with the four key objections, and presented your case from each of the perspectives.
- No one view of personality is more important than another; just learn to identify the styles which people prefer to use. Learn to move from one style to another.
- Commit to becoming extremely competent and flexible in using the model.
- A consultant who displays flexibility, and who can quickly establish rapport, will achieve much more than the consultant who relies solely on the technical merits of their proposal or their own preferred style of influencing others.

8

Consultants Implementing Change across Boundaries

A consultant needs to understand how people operate on a one-to-one basis. That was the thrust of the last chapter, with the focus on the client. In this chapter we focus on regulating, counselling, coaching and developing teams and their individual members. These are the people who are actually going to implement the solutions – the real 'implementers'. This is one of the most important issues for a consultant – they will have to energize everyone to commit to the change. In these circumstances the consultant may be running major training events when taking on the role of facilitator or trainer. Ultimately, the consultant will have to rely on their interpersonal competence, their ability to persuade, influence, negotiate and cajole others to their way of thinking. The use of position or legitimate authority will be of little value in this role. You stand or fall by your ability to present yourself, and your case, well. Remember, there will be no reporting relationship between consultants and the vast majority of the people they wish to influence. The consultant may be talking with, briefing and training a large number of people. To do this well requires an understanding of people, their aspirations, motivations and preferences for working with others and in teams.

There will be no lines of authority between the consultant and the implementers that dictate compliance. How consultants act, the skills they possess and their ability to work with a wide range of people will determine the extent to which their 'message' has credibility and is acted upon by others.

FUNCTIONAL VS CROSS-FUNCTIONAL WORK

Although we live in a world of customer-focused processes, where there is an indistinct line between functional areas, some organizations are still based strictly on the functional model. In organizational change terms it is unlikely that the consultant will be spending a great deal of time in functional silos; it is more likely that they will be working across the organization with a variety of people from different specialist backgrounds. Much internal consultancy work involves working with cross-functional teams. There can be some real benefits in addressing people from different sub-cultures within the organization, but who at the same time are probably committed jointly to improving cross-functional processes. In recent years the acquisition of team skills and the use of various team diagnostics has become critical when helping team members acclimatize to the ambiguity of virtual team working, having spent a lifetime in functional groupings.

We all strive to be team players, but sometimes the combined efforts of the group are just not realized. Often this is because the team leader has had little training in team and group dynamics. Team leaders cannot manage their teams by default. They need a variety of diagnostic tools to get the most from their people; this is where the consultant can help people to 'implement' more effectively.

There are various tools for analysis, which are extremely valuable. A simple methodology is based on the traditional 'Tuckman' model, which suggests that teams go through four distinct phases – Forming, Storming, Norming and Performing. In reality, most teams or groups don't go through all the phases to become what we would call a true 'learning team'. Too many get stuck and cannot progress to their next level of advancement.

TEAM DYNAMICS

When teams of people come together, or when people leave the team, the composition and dynamics of the team will change. The informal and formal communication networks, which have grown up and become 'business as usual', may need to change – and this is dependent upon the personalities of team members. The team may need to re-evaluate how members work together, and often this is not a conscious process driven by all the team members. Informal leadership will have its own dynamics and determine the pecking order within the group. The 'norms' within a group can change radically, either by the loss of a key or charismatic figure or by a new team member joining and influencing events.

I believe that there is lack of understanding about how teams operate, and how their 'norms' can impact (either positively or negatively) on a business. Don't believe that developing cohesive teams is critical to optimal performance. I have witnessed extremely cohesive teams of people with strong norms (which may run counter to the ethos of the business); although team linkage is high, performance is poor. This is particularly so in divisive cultures, where managers and workers are separated and a 'them and us' attitude exists. What is important is that positive 'norms' are developed and cohesive teams encouraged, and that this cohesion is aligned with the objectives of the business. It is to this end that the line manager and the consultant need to address the issue of team development.

THE FOUR-STAGE MODEL

This is characterized by four key stages. Not all teams go through the stages effectively. Here is a brief outline of the process.

STAGE 1 – FORMING

This occurs when a group (including 'virtual teams') comes together for the first time. If insufficient attention is paid to helping the team evolve in a structured fashion through each of the stages, the team will learn 'by accident' and will develop its own informal network for doing things. Not all of these 'practices' will be in the interests of team morale and corporate performance. Team members may be agreeing to an informal framework within which to perform work, but this may run counter to the mission of the organization. Here we refer to how the team will make decisions about work output based upon assumptions about people's backgrounds and their experiences. When a team is leaderless, in the formal sense, this can create a major problem. In fact, even when a team has a formal leader that team may manage the team leader rather than the other way around. Unless a team is driven by a strong individual whose values shape effective team dynamics then it will evolve by default. Sometimes the team can achieve reasonably well, but when confronted with a challenge they may not hang together, with individuals reverting to the strict demands of their job specifications. This can lead to the second stage.

STAGE 2 – STORMING

This stage is characterized by conflict and disagreement and the eventual overthrow of the old team structure and culture. The old way of transacting business may have been wrongly founded on the assumptions of team members, which don't live up to the reality of the demands on the team. During this stage major conflict may arise, especially around decision making, leadership and the use of resources. Rifts can emerge within the group indicative of several sub-cultures operating in spite of each other. This failure to work together has to be worked through or facilitated. Team effectiveness is radically reduced if no intervention takes place to introduce 'norms' – standards of behaviour that will unite the team in achieving their goal.

Old assumptions are cast aside and the team starts to learn from both its good and bad experiences. Now the team has more information about how the individuals work together as a team and this helps it to re-structure roles and responsibilities.

STAGE 3 – NORMING

As the team operates and steadily improves its ways of working, certain practices will be found to work more effectively than others. These standards and behaviours will become 'norms' for the team; these unwritten rules can frequently over-ride formal processes upon which the team should operate. Unofficial 'norms' often carry more weight with team members than formal protocols and processes. These can either be negative in origin including, for example, restricting work output beyond the group's stated norm, or positive norms such as where group members work together to protect their colleagues from excessive organizational demands.

STAGE 4 – PERFORMING

If positive norms evolve and are promoted the team will progress to become a high performance team. Where this does not happen the team leader and the consultant need to work together to diagnose the cause of the problem; they may need to go through the whole process again.

AN ADDITIONAL STAGE – MOURNING!

I have also witnessed a fifth stage, what is called the 'Mourning' stage. This often happens when teams of people are brought together to work as a special project team. They are united with a common drive and usually a target for implementation. On completion of the project they may well be returned to the function or operation from whence they came. Being chosen for the project team in the first place was recognition in itself, and may have been highly motivating, but what happens to the individual post-project? Little thought is given to re-uniting people with their old function or integrating them back into their part of the business, which has now moved on without them. This can result in a sense of loss and symptoms associated with mourning. If unmanaged, this can lead to demotivation and loss of interest in the job; people move on to other businesses. Remember, you have probably chosen high flyers to become key drivers of a project, you can't abandon them when they have achieved what you want. If 'team disintegration' is not managed, businesses could lose their best, most motivated staff to the competition. The importance of managing the transition of a project is increasingly recognized amongst virtual companies and teams.

TEAM INTERACTION

Team composition and team leadership are critical to success. The personality traits of team members are key to shaping how the team operates. Some people will tend to dominate, others will be more likely to listen and question – seeking ideas and suggestions rather than continually volunteering them. Some team members are focused solely upon task achievement while others are focused upon promoting effective harmony within the group.

Having a grasp of 'team psychometrics' is critical to understanding how the team will operate. If you can understand the dynamics of personality in the team then it is possible to predict how the team will achieve its objectives. If this is the case, then it is possible to use the strengths of the team to go on to even higher levels of performance. Using the various formats of 'team types' we can significantly – and positively – affect team performance.

This can only occur when the team is brought together and the contribution of the whole team is discussed. Each person in the team will portray certain strengths and weaknesses. Often our strengths are also our weaknesses. For example, the strengths of a go-getter who takes charge, pushes forward and is driven by achievement are soon apparent, but too much of any of these behaviours can alienate other team players. Too much drive and too much push can be perceived as abrasive and running counter to the team culture. Too much 'taking charge' can be perceived as domineering and self serving.

Encouraging people to 'look into the mirror' and become more self-critical is incredibly important in bringing together the strengths of all team members. The consultant has to win the team round to this process of self-discovery, and provide the learning to facilitate growth for the team and protection for team members who may perceive this intrusion into their 'personality type' as a threat to their self-esteem rather than a benefit to the group. There are various formats, notably that of the key originator of this concept Meredith Belbin, business school professor and author, who has long been interested in what differentiates the effective from the ineffective team. Belbin's research eventually led him to examine personality traits in a variety of management teams using one of the most reliable personality profiles, Cattell's 16 PF. From this research he distilled eight core team member types, which have further evolved to nine. (The last category is not really a team type at all but a 'Specialist' who is called upon for input only as and when required; we will not be discussing this role further.)[13] My colleagues and I also use Myers-Briggs Type Indicator (MBTI)[14] as a powerful profiling tool and the 16 'pure' types can be most powerful in understanding group dynamics. The consulting group Margerison McCann has also developed its own profiling system which draws on its own research as well as themes inherent in Belbin and MBTI. We use our own system which draws upon these three inputs and, although largely founded on the work of the above named, has some interesting insights.[15] We have attempted to align some of the aforementioned approaches in the accompanying diagram, outlining some broad similarities between set 'types'.

TEAM DYNAMICS – FOUR PERSPECTIVES

Team Dynamics Inventory (TDI)	Belbin	Myers-Briggs Type Indicator (MBTI)*	Margerison McCann
Diplomat	Chairman or Co-ordinator	ESTJ/ESFJ	Reporter-Advisor
Driver	Shaper	ENTJ/ESTJ	Thruster-Organizer
Innovator	Plant	INTJ/INTP/INFP	Creator-Innovator
Networker	Resource Investigator	ENTP/ENTJ	Explorer-Promoter
Assessor	Monitor Evaluator	ISTJ/ESTJ	Assessor-Developer
Finalizer	Completer Finisher	ISTJ	Controller-Inspector
Harmonizer	Team Worker	ENFP/ESFP	Upholder-Maintainer
Activator	Company worker or Implementer	ESTJ	Concluder-Producer

*For the Myers Briggs each of the 16 profiles is created based upon the score for the following eight dimensions, E – Extrovert, I – Introvert, S – Sensing, N – Intuition, T – Thinking, F – Feeling, J – Judging, P – Perceptive.

TEAM TYPES – WHAT VARIETIES EXIST?

There are two categories of team types – those who work on the periphery of the team (who are not always present and who may appear to take a more extroverted role), and those internal to the team (who are the real core of the team and work together). Below are the descriptors that characterize the team members.

THE DIPLOMAT

The Diplomat plays a co-ordinating and directing role. Renowned for pouring oil on troubled waters and achieving consensus, Diplomats tend to be assertive without being too pushy. The role they play will enable them to intervene, when necessary, at critical times and places, particularly if there is a point of contention. They are particularly good at orchestrating events and dealing with situations requiring adherence to protocol, which may help to dampen conflict. This is the person who controls the ebb and flow of the group and who can, when required, interject to bring other team members into the discussion. They are purposeful and adhere to agreements, always bringing discussion in the team back to the purpose of the meeting. It is said that Diplomats are neither particularly achieving nor particularly intellectually outstanding, unlike others such as the Innovator and Driver. This is in fact an important strength because they can portray a balanced approach to team discussion while being seen as an objective leader. These people undoubtedly command the respect of others and this is a critical role, which needs to be played when driving change based upon the consensus model of change.

Diplomats are excellent at sounding out the opinions of others; they rely on communication and adherence to agreed protocol to create effective teamwork. Having faith in team members, and displaying a high degree of integrity, is central to the role of the Diplomat. This indicates a tolerance for various viewpoints, which in turn reflects a nature attuned to coping, managing and directing 'diversity'. Since 'diversity' is a current issue in the way that many businesses attempt to function, the Diplomat will be a valuable member of a team. Adopting a participative approach, they are friendly, spontaneous and flexible in their dealings. Their style with people is flexible, but, in general, Diplomats tend to be tolerant and will demonstrate that they have faith in their team members.

Diplomats can be portrayed as motivators who display a high degree of enthusiasm, and this in turn promotes confidence in others. Although strongly affiliative, and exuding a high degree of self-confidence, they can at the same time disassociate or distance themselves from the front line of social conflict. They can portray the best of an orchestrator and referee, being seen to be firm but fair.

Although focused on ensuring that the team creates an effective working relationship, there is also a need to achieve desired outcomes. A positive thinker, the Diplomat with experience in a number of businesses can occupy a senior role very easily and adopt a statesmanlike position, employing people to their best capabilities – always with a goal in mind.

THE DRIVER

The Driver is so called because they have a strong desire to 'drive' events; this becomes even more pronounced if they believe that the team lacks focus. They are high achieving and motivated to get results. Drivers, like Diplomats, can be superb leaders, but their approach is very different from that of the typical Diplomat. The Driver will reach objectives by whatever method is available. In extreme cases this means that the Driver may adopt behaviour that is less than acceptable; the end justifies the means. (The Diplomat, however, is driven by more acceptable values and norms accepted by the team.) The Driver is competitive, he wants to win and will use every method available to reach this goal. The Driver will see opportunities and will have an emotional commitment to the goal; he will see it as a 'must have' or 'should have'. Frustration characterizes the Driver who is unable to reach goals, especially if the team is slow in working towards the same objectives.

Drivers are not patient enough to work well on areas such as harmonizing team morale. They will be suspicious of people who place harmony before performance. If they feel the team is not achieving they will challenge others; their sharp focus and abrasive behaviour can inhibit the team methodically working towards their objective at a slower pace. Extreme

Drivers will challenge others and be critical, and this is not always portrayed in a socially acceptable manner. Often Drivers will just 'lose it', criticizing those they perceive not to be pulling their weight. The Driver may fail to bring out the best behaviour of others in the group. This aggressive stance may create a great deal of conflict within the group. Because of their need to achieve, the Driver may appear to lack the social skills to win over others. Their directive approach may lack warmth and understanding. Undeniably, the focus of the Driver is getting results; the climate of the team is often not a consideration.

If Drivers create conflict within the group, their response to any aggression can be portrayed as humour – which is a useful way to release tension.

Up to now the picture painted of the Driver appears to be unsociable – however, there are some distinct advantages of having such a person on the team. The role of Drivers is to drive change, and they are particularly powerful in a team lacking focus and energy. They will help the team to align their thoughts and set difficult objectives. Drivers perform at their best within teams needing a charge of energy and strong direction.

A Driver's purpose is to create drive in a team, however, if this already exists then the Driver can be disruptive. If there are several Drivers in the team there will be difficulty setting direction, especially if the Drivers have opposing views. The presence of several Drivers in a team can lead to disharmony. Others in the group may not be able to handle the conflict that can often result from several Drivers competing with one another. Drivers portray the characteristics of 'aggressive extroverts', literally driven by a strong need for recognition and achievement.

THE INNOVATOR

Innovators are very different from the typical Driver. They tend to be introverted, ingenious people who are driven by their creativity. They will produce many ideas with a novel twist. They are exceedingly bright and their ideas are often imaginative and 'out of the box'. Because the ideas are so new they can be seen as impractical and untested. Sometimes the practicality of the situation may not appear to be a consideration. However, in today's climate I believe we need to encourage more people to adopt the style of the Innovator. Change is not achieved by performing the same activities and expecting a different result!

The Innovator is not a natural team player. Independent of thought and deed, Innovators will work on and develop their own ideas. The Innovator is probably best left to do this, but every effort must be made to test these ideas and ensure that they are practicable. The efforts of the Innovator should be embraced by the team; certainly, any team lacking an Innovator will fail to break new ground. In my work I have noticed a lack of Innovators in business; maybe this is because many companies have discouraged radical thought and, therefore, tended to avoid hiring or promoting Innovators to positions of responsibility. Over many years I have gathered statistics from several industries suggesting that Innovators and 'Innovator-like behaviour' are often discouraged, or at least not encouraged. Of course, there are functional areas where Innovator behaviour is encouraged including Sales, Marketing, even R&D, but generally, in the line of processing business, Innovators are seen to be too radical or unorthodox.

If a team has an Innovator then other members of the group need to make sure that their ideas are discussed and assessed critically. Here the Assessor and the Diplomat have an important role to play. Innovators can soon become disillusioned and discouraged if their ideas are ignored; they may withdraw psychologically from the team. If Innovators are very introverted they will need others in the team to bring out the ideas. If there are too many Innovators in the team ideas may never be applied.

THE NETWORKER

The Networker is another peripheral team player, spending more time generating contacts and making things happen. Networkers are the doers who make the 'strangest things happen'; they are central to any management group wanting to focus on implementation and installation. Networkers will devote their time to working out what can work and whether the resources are available to achieve objectives. Networkers may have a great number of contacts outside the team that they can rely upon to achieve the desired results. They will go outside the team and generate links with other groups if they cannot achieve results with the resources currently available. They are highly affiliative, socially confident and extroverted in behaviour, making it easy for them to become a peripheral player in several teams at once. Whereas Innovators are introverted and may appear unsociable, the Networker uses their social skills to build rapport with others in order to get the job done. This is an important asset for any team because this open and friendly manner often promotes a climate where success can be achieved.

In many teams the Networker and Innovator work well together – the Networker implementing the radical and unorthodox ideas from the Innovator. The Networker can also display creativity, but not in the same way as the Innovator. The Networker will be able to adapt applications. For example, if one approach doesn't work then Networkers will attempt another and so on until the idea can be realized. Networkers need some form of social recognition for their achievements; if this is lacking they may well turn to another approach.

Because of their social skills and ability to talk to almost anyone, Networkers will be adept at influencing and persuading others to adopt their approach, and can clearly help improve the performance of any team. However, if recognition for achievement is not forthcoming, Networkers will direct their attention to wherever and whatever receives the most social recognition.

THE ASSESSOR

Those who spend a great deal of time on the periphery of the team, for example, the Innovator, Networker and Driver, may find that their drives and needs may not be congruent. Each is driven by a different interest. The Innovator generating ideas, the Driver pushing for rapid change and the Networker using social skills to enable implementation may find that they need someone to help them get the most from their skills. Diplomats may be able to fulfill this role, but this depends upon the quality of the debate they can bring to the table. Fundamentally, someone is required to balance out the conflicting elements of the team – here Assessors can display their skills to improve overall performance and get the best from all the team.

Assessors are renowned for their intelligence and, because of their analytical ability, will display an air of objectivity. This objectivity is central to the value of the Assessor, who will not be driven by being liked or disliked but will judge things by the rationality of the argument. The Assessor will reflect on situations and analyse them dispassionately. Not being driven by subjective thoughts, the Assessor will be able calmly to appraise the efforts of team members and contribute effectively to the team. Not naturally assertive, the Assessor may adopt a background role in the team and only step forward when required, or when a situation demands a critical assessment. Because Assessors are good at assessing available options they are excellent at reaching well thought through conclusions. The role the Assessor plays in the process of teamwork is critical to ensuring that issues are debated in their entirety and sensible decisions reached. The Assessor is free from any emotional attachment to the team. The Driver wants recognition. Innovators can be easily hurt if their ideas are turned down or not implemented. Assessors, however, are objective in manner and free from such attachments; they can make an unemotional assessment.

Because Assessors are not driven by emotional considerations their analysis facilitates action within the group. Their judgement is sound and objective. However, too many Assessors in a team can stifle progress. Their cold and critical approach can sometimes dominate the performance of the team. As with all the other roles, 'balance' is the keyword.

THE FINALIZER

Finalizers dot the i's and cross the t's. They focus on the detail. They concentrate on closing loops and display their strengths by being particularly hard working and conscientious. They are excellent at picking up loose ends and ensuring that all issues are completely closed off. They are also very good at managing their time to complete 'loops'. They are good organizers and always ensure that the details and the completion schedules behind a project are finalized as required. They are committed to 'error-free work' and portray the characteristics of a 'right first time' mentality. They will exhibit strong project management skills and an ability to meet deadlines.

Finalizers will tend to express frustration if things don't go their way; they will project anxiety because they are extremely conscientious. Being naturally introverted, their emotions will not be disclosed to others. They will be focused and demonstrate a higher degree of self-discipline than their colleagues. Finalizers desire order and expect others to adhere to agreed protocols. They will stick to what is agreed and not deviate. Often, pure Finalizers will devote too much time to the detail and lose sight of the bigger picture.

Finalizers are welcome members of the team; they will augment their more radical and ideas-orientated colleagues, ensuring that plans are agreed, detailed and documented for implementation. The latter stages of any project should be left in the hands of the Finalizer who will ensure that deadlines are met and everyone is aware of their role in the final plan for implementation.

THE HARMONIZER

The Harmonizer is driven by a desire to ensure the welfare of the team. Harmonizers are concerned with developing strong psychological wellness within the team and protecting morale. They will not demonstrate an assertive role but will be seen as the 'gatekeeper' – the person who ensures that the dynamics of the team and the welfare of individuals are assessed and debated, and any improvements implemented. They put the needs of the team before their own. Harmonizers will have excellent interpersonal skills and are good communicators; they demonstrate empathy and trust and are generally sensitive in their dealings with others. They will commit more to the maintenance of the team entity rather than to achieving its 'task' objectives.

The Harmonizer is extremely diplomatic, and not being very assertive, will be welcomed by the team as a real facilitator to improve the performance of the group. They will not display a strong ambition to achieve the task – their preference is related to the internal workings of the team. Harmonizers will not embarrass other people by exposing poor performance within the team. They will not force the team to make decisions when they think it inappropriate. They are good at working through conflict and ensuring that the team reaches a win-win conclusion. They are able to deal with conflict through consensus rather than authority or dominance.

Harmonizers have excellent interpersonal skills, may demonstrate affiliative behaviour and be very out-going. They are at home listening or talking. Their natural style of actively listening while working with others will support the team in reaching a high state of harmonization.

Teams without Harmonizers will need to focus their energies on developing a degree of close teamworking, otherwise the group climate will never improve.

THE ACTIVATOR

Activators are critical to any team. The Activator is the 'workhorse' of the group, a critical member who balances the enthusiasm and 'wild ideas' of the peripheral team members such as the Innovator, the Driver and the Networker. Being conscientious, the Activator (like the Finalizer) is focused upon the detail. Activators are brilliant organizers and natural project leaders, capable of managing others to achieve a high degree of performance. Their commitment to organization and implementation is second to none. They are generally more introverted than extroverted, structured, analytical and in control of their emotions. Activators will do what they say they will do. They commit to action plans and obey any 'rules'; they adhere to structures and apply themselves in a practical manner.

The Activator and the Finalizer differ in several ways. The Finalizer is driven by an anxiety to do the job right first time and achieve closure. The Activator demonstrates little anxiety but is driven by a commitment to the organization, together with high personal standards for effectiveness. Activators are essential for balanced teamwork.

SUMMARY

Without teamwork few companies will be able to achieve a high degree of cross-functional working. This is even more important when internal consultants have to drive major changes through team cultures and large organizations. Progress only occurs when people from different silos or functions drop their functional specialisms and start working with, rather than against, each other. The failure on the part of consultants to master teamwork is a poor reflection on the skills of internal consultants within any business. It is the core role of any consultant (internal or external) to empower teams to implement solutions.

Mastering change across boundaries, working with a variety of team types on projects to resolve structural issues that can be resolved only by getting everyone to work together in one culture focused on cross-functional effectiveness, is a key challenge for all organizations. Now (and in the immediate future) 'horizontal management' of functional and cross-functional teams will be the issue that occupies the consultant. 'Matrix management' is here to stay. The concept is easily understood, but the application and installation are still a mystery to most businesses. The challenge is learning to create, and then manage, cohesive work teams.

- The consultant is ultimately measured by the degree to which they get the teams and implementers to drive change. Consultants must create a high level of team cohesion driving improved performance. Understand this; an organization that is not team driven is doomed to failure. Functional specialization will get in the way of working on improving core cross-functional processes.
- Until organizations develop recognition and progression policies into their culture, and focus completely on learning to work across functional silos, people will keep on doing what they have always done; they will put all their energies into developing their functional specialism rather than working to improve the process.
- One of the key goals of consultants is to achieve results through the team.
- How well have you, as consultant, assessed the performance of the teams with which you work? Have they successfully progressed through the four-stage model to the Performing stage?
- How well do you understand the dynamics of the teams you coach, facilitate and motivate? Have you committed to team diagnostics to assess the relative health of your team?

- What characterizes your team? Who helps and who hinders progress?
- How would you characterize key team players in all the teams with which you work? Is the composition of each team right? If not, you need to focus on minimizing weaknesses and developing the self-critical abilities of team players to work more effectively together.
- Finally, work through the dominant characteristics of all the groups and teams who use you as a Facilitator or consultant. Challenge them to work through a self-assessment of their performance and agree an action plan for change.

Implementing and Sustaining Change

As many as 90% of change initiatives fail; this is primarily because they never become part of the fabric of the organization. Unfortunately, the ideas and innovations that sparked the focus for improvement live only in the heads of the consultants and clients. These aspirations may never find their way into the culture of the organization. Success in the change cycle is determined by the extent to which change is implemented and sustained; to a large degree this is based upon focused goal setting and measuring progress. No longer can we take a leap of faith, blindly believing that things will get better. The client and consultant need to work together very closely at the first stage of the drive to ensure that their energy and vigour will gather momentum and be sustained in the months and years to come.

Research tells us that the entire change team needs to be committed to change to ensure that it lasts and creates business improvement. There must be a movement from theory to action. Hopefully, the 'implementers' have been working sufficiently closely with the consultant to make this a reality. The consultant has to be aware of other change initiatives that may be competing for resources and attention. As one [change] initiative reaches the maturity stage of its life cycle, others will be launched and begin to capture people's attention. The consultant has to make the initiative 'live'; this means continually priming the initiative from new angles, selling the benefits of change and feeding back progress reports. It is not enough to put all your energy into the launch of the change and then hope that it will gather its own momentum.

CASE STUDY

FAILING TO SPARK INTEREST OR MAINTAIN MOMENTUM

Working with a bank on a small teambuilding project I was heartened to hear that the Retail Director had recently launched a customer service drive, which had kicked off with a fanfare of PR activity and product giveaways. I looked forward to linking my staff project with the larger initiative should the opportunity arise. As I remember, over 800 people went through customer service presentations over a period of three weeks. The business was buzzing with activity and energy. As soon as the consultants arrived the presentations were delivered with gusto. After three weeks the external consultants tidied up their flip charts and OHPs and left the project for a new client. Three months later the drive for customer service was dead. No performance improvements had been registered. Little activity beyond workshop attendance was witnessed at head office or branch level. Everyone now knew that customer service was a flash in the pan. The momentum was not maintained after the initial 'smile training' workshops. No attempt was made to embed the new ideas into the fabric of the bank. No measures were in place for progress to be assessed. No one owned the programme. Small wonder the organization had difficulty persuading its people that they were serious about change.

No business can afford to introduce change in a 'hit and miss' manner. Why should staff take the issue seriously when the senior executives don't?

CREATING THE IDEAL CHANGE IN CULTURE

The end result of the launch of any change initiative or project should be the establishment of improvement processes that are visible, consistent and which reinforce the major messages of the initiative. More importantly, the change should be integrated into the fabric of normal working within the organization; it should not be seen as an activity discrete from the everyday operation of the business. To ensure that the change or project has had an impact, all relevant structures and systems supporting the project should be significantly improved. Ideally, the processes and systems should be self-sustaining, but they must be seen to be evolving to support the strategic intent of the project. How many times have changes been implemented but a clear delineation between 'business as usual' and the 'project' remains? For the project to become part of the culture it must be clearly integrated with pre-existing processes. Bearing in mind that organizations may run multiple projects simultaneously, each project will be on a different part of the project or change life cycle. As a consultant, you must ensure that these projects dovetail to create a holistic approach to improvement, rather than being seen as competing for attention, resources or expertise.

MEASURING PROGRESS – WHAT GETS MEASURED GETS DONE

Many projects, initiatives or work processes fail because the leader of the project has not defined how progress or success should be measured. What gets measured gets attention. Can you really be sure you are focusing on measuring the right things?

In this example, if a sales organization is measured on product penetration in certain markets, then that will be the focus of staff and of the resulting measurement. Here we are focusing on the 'end result' – the product penetration. What we should be focusing on is not only the results of the change but also the elements of the process of change itself. There is no point having to wait three months to find out that the end result was a dismal failure when the alternative would have been to monitor the accuracy of flows of information and the quality of decision making between key actors selling into market segments! By measuring flows and processes you design your measures to become living, breathing feedback mechanisms, not just historic data. As a result of measuring the efficacy of live processes you should be able to measure how well your database of potential new prospects has evolved. You should be able to establish the 'hit rate', the percentage of people who actually purchased the product as a ratio of the number of people targeted. Where you focus attention is what gets measured, but you must be sure you are measuring the right variables. Forget historic measures, they tell you nothing, only results at a certain point in time. Instead, focus on those activities that indicate whether or not you are achieving your goal. In the above example you would be better to focus on prospects identified as a ratio of prospects qualified.

For an HR department, consider measuring the effectiveness of training in customer management. Many would focus on the actual effectiveness of the training in changing people's perceptions of the customer, or whether they enjoyed the event, or how involved they felt in the process. Others are not interested in what people think of the event, or whether it was enjoyable and participative. I have an alternative view. I would be more interested in *tangible improvement*. For example, how did attending the event help the participants to do their job more effectively? What specific effect did attending the event have on the motivation of those attending? How did it improve individual and team performance? Did participants create an action plan during the workshop? After the event, how many discussed the content of their plan, or even the workshop, with their boss? What help, support or resource has been requested by those attending the workshop to put their ideas into practice? How many of the ideas that came out of the workshops were implemented? What impact did these ideas have on the internal supply chain? What effect, if any, has any of this training had on retaining or winning customers? What has been the impact of this workshop on staff actively measuring customer satisfaction? Is this measure ongoing, with the same customers in specific market segments? The focus here is on actions not workshop attendance, progress not participation, creative solutions implemented rather than ideas discussed!

As stated above, other measures can be used to help manage the business, but these have to be part of the cause-effect relationship in what people actually do. What causes X to happen? This is where we should focus our attention. Unfortunately, many measures used by practitioners are a waste of time. They will be of only secondary importance or will receive attention based purely upon the interest of senior management. Do senior management know how to measure people performance better than anyone else? Did they actually do the jobs for which they have created measures? For sure, only one person can define the measures by which they are assessed, and that is the person who actually does the job, day in and day out!

AGREEING MEASURES

Consultants should develop a series of measures (primary and secondary) with the support of the client. These measures should be directly linked to the business strategy and any business plan. However, if consultants have done their job well they should have won the support of those implementing the changes or the project to devise their own measures. At this stage, historic financial measures are often not what is required to drive and support the chosen strategy. It is important to identify the best measures to reflect desired behaviour changes. Nothing changes until behaviour changes. Focus on changing behaviours precisely and measures will evolve from the people who do the job, ie people will be more committed if their views on how they should be measured are incorporated into the 'actual' measures, eg customer response rates, winning repeat business etc.

BEHAVIOURAL FACTORS TO SUPPORT CHANGE

Commit time. This can be a major problem. Everything takes longer than anticipated. If everything is geared to a very tight time-frame then the chances of sustaining people's effort and enthusiasm will be slim. As a consultant you have to ensure that the change or project is of sufficient importance that, if part of the project derails, you have the time and resources to get it back on track.

Protect change champions. There will be those who are 'Early Adaptors', who take the project and drive it into the business. These people may be prepared to take some personal risks rather than wait for everyone else to come on board. As consultant, you may have to protect these people if they have incurred some risk in committing to implement the project.

Communicate and sharpen the focus. Constantly refocus attention on the overall benefits of the project and those areas which, if resources are committed, will deliver the best result for the project. Establish communications strategies that are sufficiently robust to maintain attention on the original goals for the change, and which incorporate new challenges and successes as they arise.

Reinforce behaviours that take you closer towards your goal. Establish a recognition programme that clearly articulates the behaviours required and how people will be rewarded for these behaviours. Reward progress by focusing attention on past successes and encourage people to initiate a process of 'best practice' – looking at how ideas from other areas could be made to work in their location or role.

Identify levers for change. When we examine any organizational process or aspect of a business culture there are always 'leverage points' where it is possible to gain significant advantage by applying pressure. These leverage points could be activities that potentially have a huge impact on other areas within the business, or they could be key people who, when energized, have a similar effect. Then again, they could be 'critical incidents' which, when activated at the right time, could have beneficial effects on the whole programme or project.

Many projects enter a difficult period when the measures of success have not been mutually agreed between the consultant (both internal and external) and the client. When internal and external consultants are working with a client, the internal consultant is often treated differently from the external, perhaps with less respect or trust. It is my view that the basic working relationship should be the same if the client is to achieve a successful project.

CHANGE IS A TRANSFUSION NOT AN INJECTION

This book is about change. Change can be treated as a project, an initiative or a programme. It should be managed and commitments should be made, assuming it is not a short-term project or 'quick fix' but a long-term, planned initiative that needs to be sustained and measured over time. We have focused on changing the cultural, behavioural and political landscape rather than simply addressing technical change. The change should be treated as a transfusion of energies lasting months rather than as a quick-acting injection lasting just a few weeks. A relentless commitment to Continuous Improvement must generate measures to benchmark how each business unit, function, plant or process within the organization is progressing as the project itself moves forward. Metrics should be developed between the internal/external consultant and the client; indeed everyone involved in implementing the change. Thus, we can measure our return on investment by revisiting the Rapid Improvement process outlined in Chapter 3.

SELF-ASSESSMENT – RAPID IMPROVEMENT

How would we measure the progress of leading the following stages of the change process?

Stage	Poor	Below Average	Acceptable	Outstanding
Leading the process ● Defining the project ● Client/consultant rapport – contracting roles and responsibilities ● Developing an initial plan				
Creating a desire for change ● Addressing objections to change ● Identifying resistance				

● Selling benefits ● Developing a communications strategy				
Aligning constituencies ● Working with the change team ● Dealing with resistance ● Initiating plan ● Assessing leverage for change				
Shaping an implementation plan ● Defining the path of implementation ● Focusing upon actions				
Sustaining change ● Focusing upon what you want to change ● Devising workable measures ● Setting up processes to monitor performance ● Using data to motivate and get back on course				

Hopefully, staff will have learnt from experience. Change initiatives should be geared to strategic imperatives. In the 1990s many Quality initiatives and process re-engineering events were pursued simply because the idea appealed to a key player in the management team or the concept was flavour of the month. That is why many initiatives failed. There was a failure to predict how the change would impact on the business and its performance with its customers. Many management teams committed to 'change' believing that the external consultants knew what they were doing. This was boom time for the big consultancies, launching themselves with the latest fad and undertaking major training or process improvement activities that had little impact on their clients, apart from consuming resources.

One can admire the faith of the management teams in these consultancy solutions, but often there was insufficient planning to use resources to best effect. Often the results generated were trivial and short lived. Staff may have been more aware of certain aspects of human relations and customer care but no significant change occurred. The same problems existed after the intervention, but people thought they had a handle on them because they now talked to one another! No wonder many culture change projects were seen as little more than 'being nice to each other'. Often there were no clearly defined measures by which to make change stick!

By clearly defining measures we can avoid these problems. We can track improvements in quality and reliability. We can design robust, error-free processes and deliver specific training to create specific changes in organizational behaviour. We can also monitor employee satisfaction, customer satisfaction, costs, revenue streams, the effectiveness of functions and processes, and shareholder value. We can measure anything if we start to think of the 'end in mind' as a driver, rather than an afterthought.

STARTING WITH THE END IN MIND

Careful consideration must be given to what end result is required. When 'starting with the end in mind', think about what you want your organization ultimately to become, to do and to have as assets and competencies. Only when this is clearly defined can you design an appropriate key performance measure that can be reported upon at regular intervals of time. The results must also be used as part of a carefully thought out communications process, especially to those who 'own and manage' core processes. These people must be kept abreast of everything that is happening. Don't limit your communication to the group most involved with the change initiative. Remember that everyone is part of the 'chain of change', so any initiative should be communicated widely.

CREATIVE MEASURES – APPRAISE THE CLIENT

Measurement can and should be used as part of individual and team performance agreements. Performance agreements that are formally reviewed and appraised several times a year as part of a performance appraisal process should reflect the required changes that the manager can make to promote the right culture. If we are to be serious about performance then perhaps the 'appraised' – the consultant – should also 'appraise the appraiser' – ie the client – on how well he or she supported the project. This could be a measure of the client's real commitment. Adhering to this will help keep the project on track, provide regular feedback to those affected and allow recognition – both monetary and non-monetary – to occur.

Effective measurement, tracking, feedback and communication are elements of the closed loop process that is part of any consultant's work. My experience has been that employees are not comfortable with – and do not feel part of – any project where they are not kept informed. It is important that people understand the whole picture. Allowing them to understand the measures, and keeping them regularly informed of progress through awareness and communication sessions, is critical. People need to know the 'how' and the 'why'.

CHANGE IS A CORE COMPETENCE

When measuring change it is wise to reappraise the competencies that seem to carry the most weight within the business. If a large number of competencies do not focus upon change then establish them in order to focus the attention of core managers – those who could become consultants. Understanding that 'what gets measured gets done' is a powerful way of drawing attention to several key competencies rather than a multitude of competencies, each equally graded.

BUILDING CUSTOMER FOCUS INTO PERFORMANCE MEASURES

All measures need to focus on achieving the overall goal of improved customer satisfaction. If not striving every day to improve satisfaction, retain existing and win new customers, why are we in business? For organizations in the 'not-for-profit' sector this could translate as 'value added to consumer or end user'. If we are not using our resources to make things better for the end user or the customer then we should be working on developing measures so that those people who have no opportunity to improve customer satisfaction directly and personally support those who do.

Any organization can create customer metrics to re-appraise their progress. If, for example, an organization has identified itself as not being terribly effective at 'customer responsiveness', and specific problems are identified, it is then possible and advisable to measure the transition from the 'undesired' to the 'desired' state. Focusing on our targets – the 'implementers' (as line managers throughout the whole organization) – the core responsibility is to manage this process. Each implementer will be working with a team of direct reports and be able to design specific customer metrics that report back progress. Thus it is possible to develop customer-focused measures. Through line managers and, in turn, their direct reports, an organization can develop a plethora of measures that actually reflect those areas where people can add most value. Instead of measures being imposed top-down they will arise from the work in which teams engage.

Another way of devising metrics is to answer the following question: 'How do I make a difference and add value to others in the supply chain?' Independently, business units or functions can assess their own service delivery to others in the supply chain and define metrics which reflect the priorities of these people, rather than identifying what they think is important. After an initial assessment has been made it is possible graphically to represent current 'service excellence' standards and then develop a specific action plan to move towards the 'desired state'. Measures can be easily created if you focus on what value is added to the internal customer's processes – assessed from their perspective.

CHARACTERISTICS OF EFFECTIVE MEASURES

Effective measures are:

- Time based – improvements can be specifically and tangibly measured between specified time periods.
- Visual – measures need to be easily accessed, available and transparent to those collecting the data.
- Influential – measures have to be a direct consequence of action being taken.
- Resource effective – you need to expend relatively little effort or resource to track trends in the measure.
- Relevant – the measures must be a direct consequence of critical business activity.
- Comprehensible – ease of understanding a measure that fits the 'common sense' rule.
- Aligned – the relative extent to which the measure does what it says it does.

TRAINING AND DEVELOPMENT EVALUATION

An emphasis on development training rather than action planning and results has traditionally handicapped measurement in cultural change initiatives. Consultants need to understand that any development work that is not attached to a tangible action plan for improvement will always deliver sub-optimal results. If participants on a programme cannot manage how they change and improve, then the programme's outcomes need to be rewritten. Training and development programmes are regularly cascaded down through companies with little reference to what will be achieved by attending in the short, medium or long term.

MEASURING DEVELOPMENT

Any training or development exercise should deal with challenging Attitudes, inculcating Skills and providing relevant Knowledge for those attending the programme; this is known as the 'ASK' pattern. Few programmes live up to the expectations of participants in all three areas. People often leave a programme knowing more but lacking the skills to support what they know. Similarly, very little training and development work actually addresses changing attitudes, though this can be very effectively achieved in a short period of time. It is possible to create a training climate in which beliefs and values are discussed and the process for personal 'value clarification' can be installed.

To really drive change within an organization requires a focus on changing attitudes and skills development. To ensure a focus on attitude we need to think through precisely what we want to explore, and the alternatives for participants, as well as considering the ethics in which we engage. Skills development is less contentious. Training has to be geared towards explaining what to do and also to practising that skill until it becomes unconscious, ie when you can perform the skill without having consciously to focus all your attention on its perfection. This is how we learn to drive, speak a language and play a musical instrument. The skill has to become part of 'muscle memory'. People change faster and at a deeper level if they can establish a high degree of skill in set actions. Only when that is achieved will people feel confident to go out and practise that skill.

CASE STUDY

SKILLS ACQUISITION IN TRAINING TEAMS

This project involved the training of over 30 people from a local authority housing department in Scotland, forming them into 10 teams each comprised of three people. The idea was for these teams to develop their skills in Quality and Process Improvement through a series of workshops, and then for each team to deliver tailored material to over 300 people in their business. These 30 trainees would become the 'change champions' – the internal consultants driving change. The training teams were composed of managers from a variety of areas. The purpose of this project was to install change competence within the organization so that the teams could facilitate progress over a two-year period. One of the sessions involved staff giving presentations. Out of the 30 trainees, three refused to give a 'presentation' at all, stating that they were too anxious and were not good presenters. To alleviate their concerns we focused our efforts on creating a 'safe environment' for learners. This involved starting with simple presentations lasting 20 seconds, delivered to an audience of just two people. This increased to 40 seconds with four people and then 60 seconds with six people. We spent all day taking it in turns to get participants to take insignificant risks. At the end of the day everyone in the room felt confident talking for at least 15 minutes with only the most basic prompts. At the end of the training we had 10 confident training teams. They developed confidence very quickly by being immersed in a supportive environment and being exposed to small changes involving minimal personal risk. Anyone can do, learn and improve anything if the process is designed so that they can practise their skills without being exposed to personal risk.

There are many issues that are often neglected in measuring change. I trust that the examples stated above, and some of the approaches outlined in designing suitable 'measures', will enable the development of a variety of accurate metrics for sustaining any change project.

GAP ANALYSIS

You may need to develop a more comprehensive approach to measuring improvements, particularly if you have committed to significant cultural change. Over the years my attention has been focused on using a variant of the 'Seven S's' model applied by Athos and Pascale,[16] Peters and

Waterman[17] and the consulting firm McKinsey.

The original Seven S's approach to organizational change could be broken down into 'hard' and 'soft' S's. Hard S's refers to the logical, technical, observable tools and methodologies for change; soft S's refers to the behavioural, political, intuitive, people and team elements or culture of a business. The additional Symbols, Synergy and Shared Knowledge are added to the soft S's of the original diagnostic tool for assessing organizational change. As a variant of 'gap analysis' we use the new '10 S's' framework to examine the enormity of the changes we have to take to assess whether the change we have undertaken has been successful. By listing the characteristics of the business both in terms of the hard S's – Strategy, Structure, Systems – and the soft S's – Symbols, Staff, Skills, Style, Synergy and Shared Knowledge, Sustaining Change, and Shared Values – we can draw a matrix reflecting the key characteristics of the 10 S's now and in the future.

In the diagram below, 'Application of the 10 S's Model to Assess Organizational Change',[18] we can identify with each of the 10 S's and, together with the relevant questions, can work through the action needed to move from where we are today to where we want to be tomorrow. This process is a valuable approach to diagnosing organizational health and recommending action to develop competitive advantage in the future.

APPLICATION OF THE 10 S'S MODEL TO ASSESS ORGANIZATIONAL CHANGE		
Organizational characteristics	Now, currently 'as is'	Future 'to become'
Strategy ● Where are we going strategically? ● Where are we most at risk in our core market? ● What products and services would provide security in times of change?		

Structure ● Does our structure mirror our strategy? ● How responsive is our structure? ● Where does our structure slow down responsiveness to customer needs?		
Systems ● What non-performing systems put our business at risk? ● Which processes would give us a competitive advantage as a core competence?		
Symbols ● What messages do our core symbols (such as size of office, bonuses for senior people, company cars etc) and artifacts express about how we do business? ● Symbolically, where are we weakest and strongest with the customer?		
Staff ● Which staff put our business most at risk? ● Assess the quality of people on the customer interface ● What category, level etc of personnel are we most in danger of losing to the competition?		
Skills ● What are the core competencies of the business? ● How can we stop these competencies degrading? ● What skills will put us miles ahead of our competition in the future?		
Style ● What do we require as a dominant leadership style? ● How good are our policies for retaining our best people? ● Where are we most at risk by failing to develop our managers and team leaders?		

● What is the role model for a leader, manager and team leader in our company?		
Synergy and Shared Knowledge ● Where is 'best practice' demonstrated in the business? ● Do we manage our knowledge better than our competitors? ● Have we implemented 'best practice' in our business and our industry?		
Sustaining Change ● What key initiatives would deliver our strategic objectives faster? ● How well do we manage change? ● To what extent are we structured physically and psychologically for delivering change?		
Shared Values ● What are our core values, and how well are they understood by all constituencies? ● What degree of clarity exists between our corporate values and the behaviours we reward?		

FAILING TO MEASURE THE ECONOMICS OF NON-PERFORMANCE

There are a huge number of businesses which have failed to come to terms with quantifying the economic cost associated with poor performance, frequently as a result of failing to change. These intangible costs can be extremely high, and are often costs associated with diverting people from 'value-added' to 'fire-fighting' activities. They are often not measured or monitored and never show up on a balance sheet or profit and loss account. They are the economics of reworking processes and activities that would reasonably be expected to be right first time. This simple analysis requires answers to the following questions: What direct and indirect costs are losses to the business? What are the key opportunity costs directly attributed to the failure of the business to provide services as expected?

Most organizations do not measure these non-conformance, non-compliance and non-performance costs – but they are nonetheless real. Commit to measuring costs associated with failure, whether that is cancelling a training workshop or dealing with customer complaints. A positive way of looking at this problem is to bear in mind that by 'analysing 5% of your failures comes 99% of improvement'. If a company fails to measure the costs of getting things wrong they also fail to understand where they are most at risk, and how they can prevent similar problems arising in the future.

The purpose behind this analysis is to pursue and invest in activities that would prevent these problems arising in the first place. We often find that the economics of non-performance can comprise 40% of variable costs in the service sector and approximately 15–20% in manufacturing. Most of the cost is taken up with staff having to devote their time to reworking errors and fixing things after they have gone wrong. The 'opportunity cost' of how they could have invested their time in preventing errors arising, or adding value for the business, is often neglected. By measuring the economics of non-performance, consultants can devote time to investing in prevention. The usual reason why consultants do not pursue this 'right first time' mentality is that the culture of the business is too focused on fire fighting, and too many people operate within a vacuum – dealing solely with functional issues.

SUSTAINING IMPROVEMENT

The two case studies outlined below illustrate measuring change and sustaining improvement.

CASE STUDY

EUROPEAN AUTO FINANCE

This case involves a major European manufacturer which, at the time, owned several brands of vehicles. The company provided point-of-sale finance to the dealer network within the UK. The finance company had always been successful and had operated as a centralized entity furnishing the needs of several companies. Service had never been an issue but the Managing Director wanted to streamline activities and committed to finding out what his key customers really thought about the service provided.

Although it was viewed as positive, the MD and his top team could see that a better service could be provided if they concentrated on delivering their financial products in a more focused way. After conducting a survey with the different brands we surveyed the direct reports to the top team; we then arrived at a report for improvement.

The result was a complete re-focus and re-engineering effort to re-brand Finance specifically to each of the brands. The MD and his team immediately began to work on the concept of developing 'virtual companies', providing highly specialized service to the brands with common support from the back-up functions – Credit, Legal, IT, Finance, HR and Marketing.

We created several virtual businesses, each composed of Sales and Service Account managers totally dedicated to the specific brand and dealer network. Service level agreements were confirmed, both with customers and the internal supply chain, and progress was excellent. Measures for assessing change were in place before we committed to driving the changes through the business, so that we knew we were on track.

To assess progress, a follow-up customer review was completed using questionnaires together with focused 1:1 interviews with the general managers of each of the brands. Service delivery had radically improved. We also extended the survey to the internal supply chain which highlighted areas for development and growth in the internal processing of business.

This customer service project worked. The finance company listened to the customer, restructured their business to meet customer expectations and created highly effective, sensitive, virtual businesses to work closely with the brands. Managers had new, customer-focused measures in place and benchmarked progress every six months.

A year later the new finance companies wanted to be even more self-critical and conducted their own customer surveys followed up with focus group meetings with the key managers of each of the brands. They had absorbed the capacity to change into their core business.

There have been many changes since this time with further restructuring of responsibilities as the context of the marketplace changed and adapted to growing pressure in the automotive industry. This case illustrates that – at that particular time – the company listened to the data and the diagnostic assessment, took action and sustained their drive for change. The company has since encountered many other challenges and has adapted substantially from the structure described above. What is important is that the company has adopted a 'systemic' approach to change, rolling with the markets and adapting as required. The same cannot be said of their competitors.

CASE STUDY

TECHNICAL SPECIALISM TO CUSTOMER RESPONSIVENESS

This case study reflects the work undertaken by myself with a group of manufacturing engineers in a large multinational company with HQ in Chicago. The group that committed to the change process was run by a very competent client, who had considerable experience of behavioural change. The group was highly influential as an element of the company's new product development and current manufacturing processes. It comprised 80 staff, and members of the group were very technically orientated. Most were engineers with a construction equipment, military, agricultural or automotive industry background. Many of the engineers were either new graduates or seasoned campaigners, most holding Masters degrees and professional qualifications. Intellectually, they were a powerful group with major responsibilities for managing best practice in manufacturing strategy in over 40 manufacturing facilities worldwide.

The group was founded on the need for products and services to be of higher quality, greater reliability and durability, thereby providing the customer with excellent product and service as well as creating shareholder value for the company.

The need for non-technical skill was identified as a requirement to allow the group to be more influential in process improvement. The group needed to be listened to, their suggestions recognized as valid, and they needed to be perceived as a value-adding group within the company.

Two principal actions were taken:

- A survey with a cross-section of customers, ex-employees of the group and current members of the group was conducted. Ex-employees and members of the group were key people to help test self-perception, to 'take a look in the mirror'.
- The result of the survey was a commitment to run a series of workshops designed to better equip the engineers with the ability to establish rapport and work closely with their customers. The theme of customer rapport and responsiveness would permeate each of the workshops.

This series of behaviour and learning workshops was designed and conducted by myself, the consultant. We focused on 'starting with the end in mind' when working with the client to facilitate the introduction of 'soft' skills in support of obvious technical strengths. The workshops concentrated on the most practical aspects of developing soft skills for these specific engineers. We took the content of Team Types (see Chapter 8) very seriously. The workshops focused on the role model of 'change master' in the future and the marriage of superior technical and change management skills. These workshops were strictly tailored to the client. All case material and role plays were designed to appeal to technical specialists, whose role was to influence plant managers individually to implement the ideas of this group. Sessions included 'Mastering Interpersonal Influence', 'Consulting and Diagnostic Skills', 'Addressing the Politics of Change' and 'Developing a Culture of Continuous Improvement'.

THE SURVEY

The results of the survey were fed back to all employees of the group at an off-site meeting. It took the best part of two days to feed back the data, conduct a self-assessment and discuss and agree on major steps to be taken to improve the overall group performance.

THE BUSINESS PLAN

As good business practice, and in response to their customers and the company as a whole, we developed a business plan in order to understand the role and responsibility of a business unit support function.

The plan followed the guidelines of the Corporation Quality System Procedure for a business plan. It consisted of Vision/Mission, Strategic Direction with key strategies identified, successes achieved the previous year, identification of key drivers to support the defined strategies, key measures to support the key drivers and detailed action plans. The action plan clearly identified the issue – who owned the improvement process – and the time-frames for successful improvement. (This should be basic business practice but in too many cases is not undertaken.) However, it was the client's experience that led him to appreciate the advantages of having a well-structured business plan and cascading the message throughout the organization, via a carefully thought out communications plan.

The client was a critical player in the process of change; his ownership and commitment could not have been higher. He understood that the deployment of any initiative is critical. If his people didn't know what was happening, or what was expected of them, much expert help would be lost and solutions would be less than optimum, taking too long to mature. No opportunity was lost for a structured approach to installing improvements and eliminating inefficiencies.

Upon development of the business plan a communications strategy was created for each individual customer group. A common approach to all groups of customers was resisted because of the diverse needs and cultures of these customers and the numerous interfaces served by the group in different geographies. A critical part of the business plan was the identification of key measures of performance. These had been missing previously from the focus of the group and were recognized as being critical factors in helping the group identify its value to the corporation and its impact upon business results. This was vitally important when the company focused on quarterly and annual business results of earnings per share and operating profit.

THE RESULTS

The major result was that staff in this technical role could now more successfully manage and influence the plant managers – the 'implementers'. This group had many technical features to sell to plant managers who sometimes did not share the same language. These change agents were now equipped not only with technical skill but also with change management expertise – mostly focused on getting others to implement specific manufacturing strategies from the functional grouping in Chicago.

SUMMARY

Implementing change successfully is a difficult business. In some sectors it could be claimed that 90% of change initiatives never deliver the benefits for which they were originally designed. Most failures are due to the client and consultant failing to work sufficiently close together to devise a strategy for implementing change.

If change fails it generally does so on the interface between the client and consultant. It is usually a planning and prioritizing issue. Working together to create a firm 'psychological contract' is what determines the effectiveness of change. If change fails after this, the consultant has obviously not engaged, inspired or energized the implementers.

Sustaining change requires momentum to adopt responsibilities, employ communications strategies and use feedback from measures that have been established to make change a lasting feature. We have examined the key issues in devising measures both to sustain the change and to assess the methodology employed.

- Change must become part of the fabric of the organization, it must become 'business as usual'. There needs to be a strong focus on integrating the change or project into normal working. The faster this is achieved, and new measures are put in place, the faster results will follow.
- What we focus on gets attention and closure.
- Make sure you measure the right things. Are you measuring the end results or the effectiveness of the process? Measuring the process will allow you to target, assess, redesign and fix activities as you go through the process. End result measures don't tell us what went wrong, all they provide is a historical assessment of the result.
- Always measure the effectiveness of any change activity, whether training workshops, Process Mapping meetings, project launches or communications exercises.
- Be aware of the behavioural components required to support change.
- Measure the things that are directly related to strategy and improved performance.
- Identify the required end result, and then identify the appropriate metrics. Match the metrics to what will be achieved, not to some preconceived idea.
- Communicate progress against the metrics across the whole business, not just to those directly involved with the project.
- Change is a core competence so measure the ability of your managers to drive change.
- Build the metrics into the performance agreements for the client, the consultant and implementers.
- Measure how you respond to the customer.
- If you have difficulty agreeing measures, identify what is important to your internal customer and then measure yourself on those criteria.

- Identify costs and activities associated with non-performance and measure these as an 'opportunity cost'. Replace fixing things after the event with activities to prevent problems arising.
- Survey your customers to help identify the correct strategies and business plan. This will allow you to meet your customers' requirements.
- Train and develop your people to improve performance in order to delight and satisfy your customers. Change management and technical skills are required to make sustained progress.
- Always recognize the need to review the soft S's as well as the hard S's. It is the soft S's that will have the greatest impact on staying the course over the long term; the transfusion vs the injection of change.
- Measure progress over an extensive period of time. Culture change needs a transfusion of behaviour change, not a one-off injection. Long-term passion will win over short-term projects.

Strategy for Developing an Elite Group of Change Masters

Reading through this book you will have found that progressive themes have been interwoven. I have focused on the reality that change is a political and behavioural process. I have looked at the role, the responsibilities and the interplay of the key actors in the change team – the client, the internal consultant and the implementer. Change has to be managed differently depending on where the organization is in terms of its organizational life cycle. A great deal of effort is required to devise a change process if the enterprise does not have a distinctive methodology for change. The outline of the five sequential themes in the Rapid Improvement process helped identity the core activities that need to be worked through between client and consultant. From this we moved on to a more detailed look at the Consulting Cycle, assessing readiness for change using various diagnostics to influence how the culture could be shaped to change. We also highlighted the 'dominant style' that clients display in order to give the consultant more flexibility in managing this relationship. Team types were explored in order to improve working with small groups, the implementers, and to help deal with team members, and understand their motives. We then focused on sustaining and designing measures by which to build momentum and, at the same time, review and monitor improvements.

It is important to master all these issues in order to work well as an internal consultant. The core skills and approaches have been described but we still need to outline a potential strategy that can help organizations develop their own internal capability for change.

INTERNAL CONSULTANCY

Most organizations have groups of people who occupy the role of internal consultant. But how well skilled are these people for actually driving change? We have made some assumptions about what makes a good consultant, and these themes have been explored in the book. For example, we have stated that technical competence or the use of problem-solving tools does not equate to being a first class consultant. I have worked with internal consultants who had all the knowledge of problem-solving tools but lacked the ability and personality to excite, motivate or enthuse other people to actually use those tools! One person with whom I worked was an expert in the use of 'Kepner-Tregoe' problem-solving tools but did not have the presence, or training skills, to motivate teams to use these tools.

The organization must define what it wants internal consultants 'to be' and 'to do' before setting up any structure to deliver consultancy services. Effective consultants – real change masters – may need additional skills, for example, being able to behave assertively, to lead discussions and challenge the client when required.

CHANGE MASTER SKILLS

- Interpersonal influence – know and practise strategies and tactics to influence, negotiate and persuade.
- Self-awareness and high self-esteem.
- Presentation skills – be able to talk to a variety of audiences.
- Political awareness – understand and deal with power politics.
- Assertiveness – have the ability to confront the client and others in the change team.
- Be ambitious and achieving.
- Be energetic, lively and confident.
- Be team driven.
- Address conflict.
- Be creative, questioning.

BUILDING A CHANGE INFRASTRUCTURE

We need to define what the organization requires, rather than looking at an existing support and infrastructure and trying to adapt that in some way. Many organizations have units to deal with specific aspects of consultancy, including Management Services, HR departments, Training functions, O&M, Benchmarking, Re-engineering, Best Practice managers, IT applications and support functions, Customer Relations etc. The list can be endless. These may be the exact people you need to train or, conversely, they may be the worst people to consider for the proposed change. If people are highly specialized in one discipline they may be expert in occupying a consultant role in that area but ineffective in another role. Again, we need to start with the end in mind. What types of consultants do we want to create? What is their ideal profile? What experience do they need? What are their core skills? Will this be a full-time position? If so you have a major problem at hand. Once you give someone a job title such as Internal Consultant, Quality Manager or Continuous Improvement Advisor you have unconsciously sent a message to everyone in the organization that this person or unit now has sole responsibility for that particular area of work. People see the job title 'consultant' and may think, incorrectly, that they have a very minor role to play in the change process. As soon as a 'consultancy unit' is formed in any business many managers breathe a sign of relief – the responsibility for change seems to reside elsewhere.

WHAT IS THE PURPOSE OF THE INTERNAL CONSULTANCY UNIT?

- To act as a facilitator or OD (Organization Development) consultant – as a specialist in understanding the dynamics of change – and to coach key clients and others.
- Is the change or consulting role perceived as a strategic or tactical role? This will determine where people devote their attention and refine their skills.
- To apply a particular skill that is considered a core competency

for the organization, such as Customer Management, Re-engineering etc.

- As a specialist in post-merger or acquisition situations to play the principal role in the integration of technology, processes, systems and culture.
- As a Training and Development resource – to design and deliver specific training packages across the business.
- As a problem-solver allocated to strategic projects.
- As a specialist in using particular methodologies – such as Prince 2 (Project Management Process) in the not-for-profit sector – or as an expert helping others in the business to apply for awards such as the UK's 'Investors in People'.
- To support a major change initiative, such as for the EFQM Award, and to document the application and proposal for the award.
- To act as an internal auditor who will objectively assess organizational process and issue reports and recommendations.

The practicalities of an internal 'consulting unit' can create other problems that relate to reporting relationships and funding sources. To whom does the unit submit their budget to cover the cost of their operation? Are they a profit-making business? Do they occupy more of a role of audit, inspection and control rather than pure consultancy, which is more preventative and curative in nature? Will the unit have a decision-making ability and the power to allocate funds, their time and expertise to specific strategic projects? How can their success be measured in the short and long term?

CASE STUDY

INTERNAL AUDIT – FROM TECHNICAL SPECIALISTS TO HIGH PERFORMANCE CHANGE MANAGERS

Many years ago I worked with a major utility in the UK that had an internal audit division comprising approximately 300 people. Their primary role was to provide an internal audit service to the many operations within the business. The unit actually worked well. It was very efficient in its technical role as auditors, and was an essential arm of the business, which was going through privatization. They saved the business a small fortune because they undertook the role that would normally have been outsourced to expensive external auditors. The senior management group of the division decided that, although they provided an excellent service to the business, their effectiveness could be improved.

Typically, an internal auditor would visit a business unit and conduct an audit of a particular process or aspect of that business. This could fall into a wide variety of areas, ranging anywhere from assessing the effectiveness of customer service to computer audits, financial audits, inventory management or procurement assessment etc. The auditing role was to assess weaknesses and potential problems with a particular organizational process. Having assessed the robustness of the process the auditor would then compile a report with recommendations for improvements and deliver this to the Business Unit Manager.

Working with the internal audit managers we soon discovered that, although they did a great technical job identifying weaknesses in processes, they were not measured on actually improving effectiveness. Business unit managers could agree with the internal auditor that a process they managed displayed weaknesses but take no action to improve the operation of that process. In order to improve the effectiveness of the division we had to change how the effectiveness of the internal auditor was measured. Previously, each internal auditor had been allocated work that would fill 200 working days per year 'on site' of the business unit under investigation. They were measured on the number of audits completed per year, not on the effectiveness of those audits. We changed the measures. Now the auditors would be measured against the number and quality of recommendations actually implemented per audit, rather than just the completion of the audit.

The focus of their role changed radically and, with it, their skills sets. Technical skills were still essential, but they could not do their job well without the interpersonal competence to influence and persuade others to agree and adopt an action plan to implement recommendations. This would be a difficult job for the internal auditor because their client, the Business Unit Manager, was often senior to them.

Now the 'internal auditor' was occupying both an 'analytical' and a 'change management' role. As well as selling the recommendations for the audit they also had to ensure that key actions were taken to implement their suggestions. To achieve this goal we devised a massive training exercise based upon acquiring change agent skills on two, three-day workshops – the first on 'Influencing Skills' the second on 'Consulting Skills'. All workshops were interactive with short theory inputs and intensive role plays designed and tailored specifically around influencing difficult and resistant business unit managers. The workshops were separated by 12 weeks; this time-frame enabled those attending to complete an action plan on specific activities that they had to practise in their role as advisor with unit managers.

The result was significant performance improvement within the division; the auditors started to be appreciated and valued for their bottom line contribution to the business. The division acquired considerably more political clout with others in the business. However, we also found that staff turnover in the unit increased; this was initially unsettling until we discovered that managers throughout the whole business viewed the Internal Audit function as a great breeding ground for high flyers. Staff who located to the Internal Audit Division soon gained a depth and range of experience in the business and became an attractive commodity to the rest of the organization. The managers of the division took this as a compliment and worked with their people, knowing that they would be going on to highly valued and well-rewarded line management positions within the company. This was great news for the profile of the division because this knowledge was hard to contain and soon ambitious staff would almost be guaranteed speedy promotion after working in the division.

A key learning point from this case is that the management group of the division produced a significant shift in the culture of the business, from initially being seen simply as an overhead, as a division that used their technical detail to avoid unnecessary external audit costs, to a division that thrived on implementing change and providing the business with high flyers with great experience in a short period of time.

If an internal consultancy unit does not exist within an organization it is generally not a good idea to introduce one unless there is a specific need. I have witnessed some businesses creating a special consulting unit to focus specifically upon developing and implementing a post-acquisition integration strategy with another business. Other units have been created to deal with fairly discrete problems such as IT initiatives or major 'critical incidents' where the growth or survival of the business may be at risk. It is usual for these units to be highly controlled and specific in focus. What we need for the average business is an ethos and infrastructure that is 'virtual' in nature, and easily redesigned, reformatted and re-invented to meet its changing agenda.

If some form of consulting unit already exists then it may be possible to build it into what the business really desires. A major problem here is assessing whether the history of the unit, and its relative effectiveness, could create negative perceptions with some people. If the historic record of the unit's success is limited or negative no amount of change or improvement will dispel the image. Likewise, if the calibre of the people running or working in the unit is less than competent to meet the expectations of the client then it may be better to build a different structure. Will the unit be expected to deal with strategic, long-term global issues or tactical, short-term local issues? The history of the unit will tell you which solution is more appropriate.

Another major problem with creating such a unit is the perception of senior management. Will they see the consulting group or unit as the main or sole vehicle to initiate and drive change? This attitude, if allowed to persist, reinforces the view that change is the responsibility of 'other people'. The same view prevails in organizations where HR or Management Services have provided similar services in the past. It is too easy to relegate change to a specialized grouping or function. The worst example I came across was in a software development business whose Personnel function was renamed 'Change Management'. The technical specialists occupying other functions clearly had a ready-made excuse to side step change, especially when a function was named after the process itself!

Another problem with having a specialized change or consultancy unit is its funding and role in the enterprise. If a separate consultancy unit exists it must have a purpose and be strongly linked to the strategic direction of the organization.

Employing a core of 'change specialists' in this function means that their expertise for implementing change may reside solely – and be contained strictly within – the confines of the unit. This can create problems with an elite group who are perceived as being separate from the rest of the organization. It is almost as if they are assumed to have access to 'mystical' processes which enable them magically to create change. Access to an inner sanctum controlled by special knowledge and experience makes consulting seem even more like a dark art! Change is an organizational issue and should be spread right across the business. If a consultancy unit does exist it should be easily accessed and its role clearly understood by others. The easier the access the more internal consulting practice will spread in the company.

However, you may not have agreed yet on a structure for the provision of a consulting group or infrastructure. A compromise may be appropriate, such as the consultancy unit being headed up by only one full-time manager of good reputation and track record in driving change. The unit is then driven by high calibre people seconded to the unit. These high flyers must have specialist skills or experience or their secondment will be perceived as a 'development opportunity' for their further advancement in the business.

Taking this idea further, an ideal arrangement may be for the unit to be a 'virtual' business that is headed by the CEO or chairman of the business as a caretaker client overseeing all strategic change. What messages do you think this would send out to the organization about the importance and achievement of competency in consulting skills and change management? All the CEO would need to do is ensure that the unit was funded and the positioning of the CEO as leading the 'virtual' unit would demonstrate the relative commitment given to various strategic projects. This 'informal arrangement' is what occurs in many organizations today. The CEO often decides on implementing a 'set process' and then takes responsibility by winning support from 'talented, motivated and ambitious' staff to drive the project to speedy implementation. It is no surprise to find that in most businesses the same people are 'reprocessed' and used time and again as internal consultants. This indicates several problems, the biggest issue being, why has the organization such a small number of talented people to call upon to implement a special project? This question should encourage the organization to equip more line managers with the change master mindset and competencies.

The final issue reinforces the points made above. If the business allows a separate change or consultancy unit to exist outside of the main operation of business does this diminish the notion that change is the responsibility of line management? This needs to be thought through carefully. But just consider the benefits of having a team of managers ready and able to manage most issues of change management. What would it mean for your business to have managers equipped with the consulting know-how to impact on improvement? Having the skills and expertise to change oneself and others should be a core competence for any business.

Generally, we get the supervision and managers we deserve. If we fail to develop people, for example line managers as change agents and internal consultants, we inhibit the contribution of our best people to the business. If we have a culture staffed mostly by managers who lack the talent and enthusiasm to act as consultants for new projects or initiatives, where does the fault lie for this lack of vision?

CREATING INTERNAL CAPABILITY FOR CHANGE...

Any senior team that believes that the technical expertise of their employees represents their total contribution to the company has much to learn.

Managers need to understand more about the dynamics of change and how to influence employees at all levels within the organization. People resist change for many reasons, but the change process should not be a mystery to them. Exploring the change process from both a personal and organizational perspective will have many paybacks. Those who become change agents or consultants will stretch themselves and achieve a new-found confidence. Confident managers and employees are very powerful. They start taking a new interest in how things happen, and when they develop this curiosity they become even more keen to see how things could be better organized.

I have yet to find managers who have not personally improved their perception of how they manage, influence and get others to commit to change after attending our programmes. Our goal is to ensure that, after contributing and learning through the workshops and our methodology for change, managers find it hard not to add value to their business and their self-esteem!

DESIGNING A CULTURE DRIVING RELENTLESS IMPROVEMENT

There is no secret system that has been saved for the last few pages of this book. The process that I continue to use is refined and improved every time it is applied, tailored to the needs of the organization. This tailoring depends upon the organization's constraints and demands and the place it occupies in the organizational life cycle. The process will work because you have to start where the organization currently stands in its quest for improvement. The strategy starts where the organization, location or operation currently is in terms of 'change maturity', not where we or others would like it to be.

HOW READY IS THE BUSINESS FOR SUSTAINING A STRATEGY OF CHANGE MASTERY?

To start the process you need to examine the relative health of the business, using several instruments to assess the readiness of the corporate culture for change. This analysis should be delivered 'speedily', with no time wasted between data collection, analysis and action. All activities, especially the design of the 'diagnostics', must be bespoke to the organization. Winning the commitment of the 'top team,' the 'big hitters' or dynamic leaders who want to improve performance radically by using key managers as change agents is critical to this process.

The data are collected and diagnostics applied and fed back to the top team and clients; issues are discussed using the 10 S's framework discussed in Chapter 9. The top team uses a template and scoring system to identify the priorities to be resolved to equip the business with the necessary degree of change competence. The team then commits to a very detailed and sequenced action plan for implementation, which is time bound and reviewed at regular intervals.

COMMIT TO TRAIN DIRECT REPORTS

At this stage the top team has recognized the importance of their managerial group as 'change masters'. They then have a choice; do they pick a group of managers from various locations and functions to undertake the process or do they commit to a braver solution? Do they commit to training their direct reports and other managers at a senior level? The advantages of this approach are obvious and are concerned with moving managers beyond their narrow, technical comfort zone. If an organization cannot utilize and develop the top two or three tiers of management to become effective 'change masters' or 'consultants' they are probably functioning sub-optimally.

Organizations need to commit to learning, experimenting and applying best practice in change management and consultancy interventions, focused upon change management and interpersonal competence. This will help managers competently improve and impact positively on the business.

Once managers are competent in the dynamics of the change process, and the use of specific tools, they are formed into change teams organized on a cross-functional basis. As a change team they will meet to assess how best to install a commitment to building a culture of change and improvement within their operations.

'CAN DO, WILL DO'

Fundamentally, there are two key forces within any business that determine the degree to which change can be implemented effectively. The most important is the force or energy that people at all levels display and radiate. It is the role of the consultant or change agent to work on raising that energy. This will never happen without a 'can-do' mindset and culture. It is founded upon a firm commitment to drive change; it challenges the old ways and replaces them with rigorous, innovative and vibrant solutions implemented without hesitation. If the consultants have done their job properly they will have revitalized the hearts and minds of the people at all levels. To be really successful in driving change demands an enormous amount of personal energy, which is overpowering in its intensity and focus. Energy is reflected in people's level of activity and forward thinking, which reflects their degree of self-esteem and their focus upon achievement. Consider the alternative – a large bureaucratic structure that emits a trickle of energy reflecting its poor capacity to act. The real energy comes from those who want to drive change and are committed to transformational leadership. Their energy is reflected in the passion and enthusiasm of the people who drive the culture. A slow-moving organization is probably managed by equally slow managers who have little energy and commitment to business improvement.

Energy is not the only requirement. Boundless energy is of little value without focus, and does not guarantee success. Ensuring that there is a strong direction reflecting a vision for the business to gain and practise 'change mastery' is the core value for people committed to improvement. This value is lived in the fact that focus, passion and energy are all aligned.

CONSULTANT SKILLS – KEY FACTORS FOR CHANGE OR PROJECT IMPLEMENTATION

● Effective, speedy change is based upon the existence of a shared 'desire' among the key players in the process, and this should demonstrate that they really want and value the end goal.

The 'implementers' who articulate the goal should be enthusiastic and express their personal commitment to the change or intervention with passion and enthusiasm. A damp squib reaction is of little value. If the goal of the project or change is not compelling, or is vague, then it is unlikely to be achieved. If the goal is vibrant, bright and easy to understand – and represents the feelings of the company – then it will be embraced.

- Consultants have to truly believe that the company and staff have the ability to achieve the goal. This goal has to be realistic, it must fit within certain constraints and be supportive of the company vision and strategy to which the consultants require access. Sometimes consultants fail to focus upon challenging goals and instead focus too much on the detail of the project. They fail to stretch themselves beyond their experience and corporate comfort zone. Individual ambition and self-confidence on the part of consultants can create self-limiting beliefs, which constrain choice, challenge and creativity.

- Change goals must be written down in accessible language. For example, the vision of Pepsi to 'beat Coke' is instantly understandable. Simple goals are visual and can be easily understood by anyone in the organization. The more specific the better – defined in precise terms.

- Define now how you will benefit from achieving the project outcomes. Focus upon exploring and communicating the benefits of the change to everybody. This is a key area for improvement in most businesses. Having senior staff articulate the short and long-term benefits of the corporate change from a business, shareholder, customer and staff perspective is key if people are to understand why you are pursuing the required changes. The more benefits that consultants can encourage senior managers as clients to articulate and communicate to key constituents the better. If they can only find one or two benefits, which accrue to the business and shareholders only, it is unlikely that employees will buy in to the process with enthusiasm. It is the consultant's role to equip managers with an understanding of how to use the tools of communication.

- Assessing the time needed to achieve key milestones in the project is dependent upon the relative health of the organization. Managing the gap becomes easier if there is a clear understanding of the steps to be taken. If you are a long way from achieving your goal then you need to break down transitions into discrete steps, which become sub-goals; their achievement becomes the foundation for incremental change.

- Set a deadline for the completion of the projects or sub-projects and review these continually. Strong, effective project management is essential for maximum success. Adopt a critical attitude and understand now whether you are getting closer to, or further away from, your goal. You will need measures to assess progress. Make sure your goals are tangible and quantifiable.

- Identify the key barriers to achieving your goal and the key players in the organization who can help you – either to facilitate change or to open doors. Discover the opinion formers and align yourself with them in order to win their support.

- What knowledge will you need to help yourself and others achieve your project? Who is important in the power stakes, and how reliable and resilient are they in their support of you and your team?

- Have a clear image of achieving your goal. It is a good idea to describe how things will change, and what will be the core characteristics of this change. Imagine what others will see – what will be different – what others will say and what attitude they will display. How will people feel about the changes?

- Win the support of others to write a detailed action plan reflecting roles, responsibilities and ownership. Too many implementation plans remain within the heads of senior managers or the implementation team. When writing about achieving the goals write about them as a certainty.

DEVELOPING CHANGE MASTERY

If there is any magic in change mastery it is in designing learning experiences specifically to the context and challenges that participants will actually encounter. There is nothing magical about the content of any of the material, except that it is focused on what really happens in the change management process. This means bringing out the reality of the politics of change. It means exploring the mixed motives and relative power of the key actors in the process, some of whom may be orchestrating events while not even being physically present to discuss their positions and intentions.

Instead of focusing upon tools for improvement and problem-solving technologies that we can access from CDs and the Internet, we work on creating a strong culture of teamwork. We do this in a very tangible manner so managers can assess how they are doing, and how they have improved week by week.

Learning materials and manuals are focused upon processes and are cultural, behavioural and political in nature.

If there were any secrets to change mastery where would you find them? Answer these questions.

On the process of change – personal skills:

- What is change and what are the stages of change?
- How do I change?
- Why do I resist change?
- If I were to design a perfect 'me' what would I change?
- Why do others resist change?
- What strategies can I practise to support others to implement change?
- What is my strategy and preference for managing conflict and ambiguity?
- What are my preferences for influencing others?
- What do I consciously and unconsciously communicate to others?

- What other strategies for influencing others could I employ?
- What are the six strategies for change that work every time?
- How can I take charge of the communications process?
- What elements of 'hypnotic language' patterns (such as the use of certain exciting, active and positive words or phrases) could improve my hit rate when presenting to others?
- How can I better read the intentions of others through their posture?
- How can I become better at changing those things that need to be changed about me?
- How can I manage change with others more effectively?
- How can I motivate others?
- How can I inject a high degree of energy into teams?
- How can I present with power?
- Why is behavioural change so important?
- How do people change their behaviour?
- How can we encourage others to develop a self-critical view on improving performance in how we work with, manage and innovate with others?

On the process of leading change through others:

- How well do I know and manage my client?
- How can I develop a strong psychological contract with my client?
- How can I better prepare to avoid unnecessary conflict with clients and implementers?
- How does our change team interact with others, and how can we improve our performance in designing the chain of events to ensure change actually happens?
- Which areas of the change process or 'change path' demand extra attention and which unclosed loops create most problems in terms of implementation?
- How can people work more effectively in functional, cross-functional and virtual teams?

- How can we create a planned and preventative strategy where energy is concentrated on how to create synergistic relationships and results?
- How can I improve my personal performance and enhance my creativity and innovation towards my team and my colleagues?
- What do I need to learn and how can I enable others to learn those things that will enable them to achieve their potential?

SUMMARY

Starting with the end in mind is key to any change initiative. If you are thinking of developing a team of internal consultants or change masters, what do you want the consultants to actually do? Do you have an existing structure for change implementation? If so, how effective is it? Have you considered the effects of creating such a structure? Have you considered alternatives such as a 'virtual' consulting? What are the core skills of the consultant? Do you have a role model for the ideal consultant? These are all issues that require the input of the organization.

Building internal capability for change requires a major investment in planning and a focus on developing a solid ethos within the organization of 'change is the culture'.

Notes

Chapter 1 – Change as a Political and Behavioural Process

1   *Why Quality Fails* report, Genesis Consulting Group, Geneva, 1990.
2   *Making Mergers Work*, Price Pritchett, McGraw-Hill, 1987.
3   *Understanding Organisations*, Charles Handy, Penguin, 1976.
4   Raven and French – 'Legitimate Power, Coercive Power and Observability in Social Influence', *Sociometry*, 1958.

Chapter 3 – The Internal Consultant Developing a Methodology for Change

5   'Unlocking the Secret behind the Balanced Business Scorecard', Philip Atkinson and Malcolm Holden, *Journal of the Institute of Management Services*, May 2000.
6   Dr W Edwards Deming – Quality guru who taught the Japanese all they knew about Quality, author of many texts on Quality Management – who failed to be taken seriously by his own country, the USA, who thought that Quality was not a key issue in the strategic management of business.

Chapter 4 – The Change Team – The Role of the Internal Consultant and Client

7   *Managing at the Speed of Change*, Daryl Conner, Wiley, 1997.

Chapter 5 – Action Research – The Consulting Cycle, Psychological Contracting

8   'Action Research' as a methodology was developed by Reg Revens.

9   *Organizational Psychology*, David Kolb, Prentice Hall, 1984.

Chapter 6 – Cultural Analysis

10   *Understanding Organisations*, Charles Handy, Chapter 7 on 'Structures and Cultures', Penguin, 1976. Many revisions since this time.

11   *On Death and Dying*, Elisabeth Kubler-Ross, Scribner, 1997.

Chapter 7 – Assessing the Style of the Client

12   'Personality and Objection Handling Inventory', Philip Atkinson, 1990. Developed from a variety of earlier models – ie the Wilson Corporation USA, Thomas International PPA Profile etc.

Chapter 8 – Consultants Implementing Change across Boundaries

13   There are certainly many people in industry who fall into this mode and their preference for working with a team as an 'outsider' to the team must be valued and respected. However, the success for most enterprises rests on creating high performance teams rather than individual specialists working independently.

14   Katherine Cook Briggs and Isabel Briggs Myers.

15   'Team Dynamics Inventory' (TDI) ©, available from the author, Philip Atkinson.

Chapter 9 – Implementing and Sustaining Change

16   *The Art of Japanese Management*, Athos and Pascale, Simon & Schuster, 1981.

17   *In Search of Excellence*, Peters and Waterman, Harper & Row, 1982.

18   Philip Atkinson Consulting – Diagnostic: Culture Change. An excerpt from a 100 item questionnaire. © 2000.